Soldiers of Napoleon

Soldiers of Napoleon

The Experiences of the Men
of the French First Empire

Under the Eagles
A. J. Doisy de Villargennes

Voices of 1812
Arthur Chuquet

LEONAUR

Soldiers of Napoleon: The Experiences
of the Men
of the French First Empire
Under the Eagles by A. J. Doisy De Villargennes
Voices of 1812 by Arthur Chuquet

First published under the titles
Army Life under Napoleon
and
Human Voices From the
Russian Campaign of 1812

Leonaur is an imprint
of Oakpast Ltd

ISBN: 978-1-84677-576-5 (hardcover)
ISBN: 978-1-84677-575-8 (softcover)

http://www.leonaur.com

Publisher's Notes

In the interests of authenticity, the spellings, grammar and place names
used have been retained from the original editions.

The opinions of the authors represent a view of events in which he
was a participant related from his own perspective,
as such the text is relevant as an historical document.

The views expressed in this book are not necessarily
those of the publisher.

Contents

Under the Eagles

A. J. Doisy de Villargennes

Contents

Preface

Some six or seven years since, my father, at the request of a member of his family, undertook to write down a few recollections of his former career while serving in the army under Napoleon.

This work does not pretend to be a connected history of that period. As its title indicates, it is merely a series of reminiscences of events mostly within the experience of the writer; events which had impressed themselves more forcibly upon his mind than did other occurrences of equal or perhaps superior importance.

At the time of writing these memoirs, the author was about eighty-four years of age, but his memory was unimpaired in regard to all matters relating to the early period of his life. The strong grasp which the young mind had fastened upon the then present events had never released nor even slackened its hold, although the matured memory was dropping daily from its clasp, the more recent occurrences of life.

In the month of August, 1869, the one hundredth anniversary of the birth of Napoleon was celebrated with great enthusiasm by the French citizens of Detroit, Michigan. My father made the closing speech of the occasion; its peroration is here quoted as being a good exemplification of the ruling passion which ran through his life, and was strong even to the end:

> I never took any other oath of allegiance but that of fidelity to Napoleon and his dynasty; that oath I have kept; I shall keep it. I never uttered but one political exclamation,

and it, I hope, will exhale itself with my dying breath: '*Vive l'Empereur* Napoleon!'
L. A. J. D. (Z. Z.)

Memoirs

The stirring events of the first decade in the present century were calculated to launch youth prematurely into the troubled ocean of man's life. I seem to have been destined to follow the tide. At the age of fifteen years I began the world on my own individuality. A tradition in our family asserted that one of its ancestors had been an admiral; this, possibly, together with the fact of my own adventurous disposition, influenced my parents' decision in regard to my future destiny, and it was settled that I should enter the navy.

In November, 1807, the Emperor Napoleon Bonaparte resolved to wrest Portugal from the domination of England, and sent for this purpose an expedition commanded by Junot. In the harbour of Lisbon was found a small fleet, which the escaped family of Braganza had no time to take away with them to Brazil. The command of this squadron was given to Commodore Magendie, a distant relation of my mother, and he took me with him as his secretary, although I was nominally enrolled as a novice on the books of the Vasco de Gama, the flag-ship. During the nine months, however, that our army occupied Portugal, I was but three or four times on board.

I may here state that my appointment as secretary was due, not only to family interest, but to my reputation among admiring friends as an English scholar; for had I not gained a premium at school for my extemporaneous translation of a page of Goldsmith's Vicar of Wakefield? Did I not glibly enough repeat from my book of dialogues such sentences as the following, pronounced, too, as I endeavour here to represent them: "Good mor-naing, sair. Haou do you do? Zis is bioutayfool oizer," etc.

After the battle of Vimeira and the convention of Cintra, our army was conveyed back to France in English vessels. But before leaving the Tagus, I must relate a comical incident, which might, however, have had serious consequences.

On the eve of sailing, General Laborde invited several English army officers, from whom he had received attention, to meet at dinner some French officers who were on board with him; as a compliment, he invited likewise a navy officer named Garrott, who acted then as Agent of the Transport Board. This latter was a little, vulgar man, who, whenever he had the opportunity, lost his reason in his libations. Commodore Magendie and myself were also of the party, and on account of my knowledge (?) of English I was placed near Captain Garrott, to serve as interpreter, if occasion offered.

It was then the 3rd of September, and the stern windows of the cabin were left open on account of the heat. The dinner passed on pleasantly, and friend Garrott paid assiduous court to the bottles within reach. When the fruit was laid on the table, General Laborde rose, filled his glass, and in a short, appropriate speech, proposed the health of his Majesty, King George III. The toast was drank with enthusiasm, the whole company standing. Then an English officer (Colonel Haverfield, I believe) rose, and in courteous terms proposed the health of the Emperor Napoleon.

All glasses were cheerfully emptied, except that of Garrott, who began to protest vociferously, in language wholly unbecoming a gentleman, that he never would drink to the health of "Boney." On the other side of me was seated a French major of cavalry, Petit by name, a man of Herculean size and power. To this gentleman Captain Garrott now began to address his conversation, if such could be called the volley of oaths and senseless curses with which he seasoned his discourse, until at last he roused the indignation of the English officers.

Major Petit had heretofore remained imperturbable, but now, at an insulting gesture of Garrott, he rose, saying coolly, "Gentlemen, be pleased to leave him to me." Upon which he went to Garrott, seized him as he would a doll, by the collar and trousers, and walking to the window, balanced him for a moment, and then deliberately pitched him into the Tagus!

Turning to the company: "Gentlemen," said he coolly, "if any one is dissatisfied, I am at his service."

Several voices at once, accompanied by loud laughter, called out, "No, no! Well done! Served him right!"

Meanwhile, poor Garrott was fished up by the crew of a boat moored astern of the ship, and returned all dripping to the cabin; apparently sobered, and giving no sign of displeasure at his strange visit to the Tagus.

Poor man! I should not speak lightly of him, for I owe him a debt of gratitude. Endowed with a sort of faculty or instinct, which enabled him to comprehend, or rather to guess the meaning of my language, he proclaimed me to all comers as a very satisfactory English scholar, and thus propped up my reputation, sadly shaken, if not wholly demolished, by an incident that occurred about this time.

A commissary in the English army having occasion to obtain some information from the commodore, called at our office, and his French being found unintelligible, he was referred to me. Our conversation must have been, to him at least, little edifying or satisfactory, for at last he concluded by saying in very bland tones: "My dear young friend, I wish you would talk French; I may perhaps make it out better than your English!" I was simple enough to rehearse this compliment among my acquaintances, and thereby drew upon myself sarcasm that tended not a little to crush whatever degree of conceit had been in me.

Shortly after my return to France, I was shipped on the frigate *Pallas*, where I passed my examination, and became a midshipman. On the night of April 11, 1809, the blockading English fleet sent fire-ships through ours, then at anchor. A few days after this event, I was surprised at receiving a commission as sub-lieutenant in the 26th Regiment of Infantry, then at Strasbourg, on its way to Germany, with orders to join it immediately. My father, without consulting me, and foreseeing quicker promotion in the army than in the navy, had obtained this commission for me. My regiment arrived at the island of Loban in time to share in the battle of Essling, May 22nd, and in which, as my baptism of fire, I was wounded by the splinter of a shell.

In speaking of this, my first campaign, I shall abstain, for two reasons, from attempting to describe any of its varied engagements. First, I witnessed but few of its numerous skirmishes; second, I do not wish to resemble those who, on the plea that they were present at a battle, pretend to give an accurate account of the action; their very presence precludes their ability to present such a report. I speak, of course, of inferior officers only; they, indeed, can portray the evolutions of their own corps; the sudden passage of a battery of field artillery, or the momentary charge of a body of cavalry, etc. But the noise, the cloud of smoke, the agitation consequent upon each one obeying implicitly orders of which, perhaps, he does not understand the bearing; the extent of the field, sometimes, as at Wagram, covering miles; every circumstance, in short, tends to incapacitate the subaltern from filling faithfully the office of a reporter. Speaking for myself, I declare that after an engagement worth the appellation of a battle, I have invariably learned the particulars of it two or three days later from the bulletins of head-quarters.

Instead of venturing to discuss subjects beyond my power, I shall meet the object and the title of this narration better by relating two incidents which occurred in the course of this short campaign, premising that I did not witness either of them, but that they were the universal and uncontradicted subject of conversation in the army, though, for obvious reasons, publicity in the newspapers was suppressed.

After the battles of Eckmuhl and Ratisbon, a magnificent avenue leading to the latter city had been totally ruined by the passage of upward of two hundred thousand men. The emperor ordered it to be repaired, and a company of infantry was posted at each extremity, with the express command not to allow any one to enter it on horseback. General Vandamme, as well known for his bravery as for the extreme rudeness of his manners, presented himself on his horse at the entrance of the avenue, and was proceeding further, when the sentry on duty, a raw young recruit, came forward and stated the orders he had received.

"GeneralVandamme passes anywhere!" exclaimedVandamme; "get out of the way!" On the soldier's appearing to insist, the general gave him a blow of his whip across the face, cursing his impudence.

The young lad, intimidated, was about to yield, when the captain who commanded at the post, and who, walking about, had witnessed the scene, rushed toward the sentry, snatched the musket violently out of his hands, and, running in front of the general, levelled the piece at him, exclaiming, "General, if you advance one step more I will shoot you like a dog for daring to treat my sentry as you have done!" Vandamme, seeing at once whom he had to deal with, thought it best to comply, and withdrew, muttering a threat to revenge himself on the bold captain.

An opportunity soon presented itself. General Vandamme, being the temporary governor of Ratisbon, on visiting the different posts, recognized in the officer on duty at the main guard on the great square of the city the unlucky captain who had checkmated him at the avenue. The square was then swarming with lounging officers of all ranks. Vandamme took no apparent notice of his adversary, but having fully recognized him, went away without addressing him a word. Soon, however, profiting by the vicinity of a small crooked street, such as are almost all streets in Ratisbon, he suddenly reappeared before the post. The sentry immediately called out the guard, according to regulations when the commanding general presents himself. The captain instantly rushed out with the guard, but so sudden and unexpected had been the second visit of the general that a few minutes elapsed before the ranks were formed and arms presented.

Meanwhile, the general, standing motionless, had waited for this moment; then, giving vent to his brutal disposition, he assailed the unfortunate captain in the most opprobrious terms, telling him that he was fitter to drive a herd of hogs than to command soldiers, etc. By this time a crowd of officers had collected round the spot. The captain, during this painful scene, had sufficient control over himself to refrain from answering a single word. But, as soon as his post was relieved, he called on Marshal Oudinot, the commander of the staff, and, after relating the facts of the affair, demanded permission to challenge General Vandamme. The marshal, in rather severe tones, refused the request. On this the captain (his name was, I believe, Jollivet, 14th Light Infantry) did not hesitate a moment, but aware, as was all the army, how easy of access the emperor was, he at once determined on having direct recourse to his majesty.

He accordingly repaired to the pavilion occupied by Napoleon, demanded and obtained an immediate audience, related in the fullest details both his interviews with General Vandamme, and concluded with a request for the same favour which he had vainly solicited from Oudinot. Napoleon, with his usual affability toward his inferiors, answered: "Sir, I sympathize with your feelings on this occasion; but you must feel that your demand is inadmissible. The general officers of the army are to be here tomorrow at twelve o'clock—come at the same hour. Meanwhile, I shall have strict inquiry made; and if, as I do not doubt, your version of the affair is quite correct, I shall require a suitable apology from General Vandamme to you."

Punctual to the hour, the captain attended the meeting, and modestly, from the inferiority of his rank, remained behind the circle formed round the emperor. The conversation, as on such ceremonious occasions, was confined to trivial subjects, and the company seemed preparing to take their leave, when our bold captain, elbowing his way through marshals and generals, stepped into the centre of the circle, and fearlessly addressing the emperor, said: "Sire, you vouchsafed to promise me you would demand from General Vandamme, here present, some apology for the undeserved insults which he offered me. I come here in consequence of this promise."

Napoleon, without answering the captain, turned to Vandamme, saying: "General, I have inquired into the facts of this disagreeable affair, and I find that you have most unwarrantably and outrageously insulted an officer who enjoys in his corps the highest character. You owe him a suitable apology, as public as your insult has been, and I insist on your making it here."

"Sire," answered Vandamme, "I must regret having been carried away by passion in my addressing Captain Jollivet; but these gentlemen"——

"That's enough!" exclaimed the captain. "I am satisfied. Sire, I owe you more than my life. I thank your majesty." He could say no more; emotion had stifled his voice; he bowed and retired. I have not heard what his subsequent career may have been.

It frequently happened that sudden acclamations of "*Vive l'Empereur!*" stirred the humours of our bivouac fires. This often occurred from the enthusiasm of the soldiers at the recital of some trait in the life of their idolized chief. The first outpouring of such a feeling witnessed by me was occasioned by the animated account of the foregoing incident by a sergeant to a large concourse of soldiers. The strict sense of justice; the generosity of Napoleon toward those who had served well, or toward the families of those who had fallen; his paternal attention to those in hospitals; his severe surveillance over the conduct of contractors for the supply of the troops; the commanding influence which he unaffectedly exerted over his most distinguished generals; all these aroused the enthusiasm of our soldiers at the mere recital of some agreeable trait in the acts of their idol.

I feel a certain reluctance in relating the second incident alluded to above, as it affects a character for which I profess and entertain the highest respect: that of a French officer. But there are in all armies a few individuals unworthy of the epaulettes which they wear; and the publicity given to the unmasking and punishing the man who has disgraced his rank is a lesson of public morals which may have more than one useful application.

While a part of the army was at Passau, at the confluence of the river Inn with the Danube, a major in the artillery of the

Imperial Guard (I shall suppress his name) had acquired a most detestable notoriety by the number of duels, by him styled successful, which he had fought. His skill with sword or pistol, as well as his insolence, had become proverbial, and his comrades had nicknamed him "*Le grand diable.*" One day, at a coffee house much frequented by officers, two captains in the 65th of the line had been there playing a game of billiards. One of them, having momentarily left the room, his friend was awaiting him, standing near the table.

At this moment in stepped the major, accompanied by two friends. Approaching the table he took up the balls, and was proceeding to arrange them anew when the absent gentleman returned and interposed, stating in polite terms that the table was engaged, as he and his friend were then in the midst of a game. "I insist," exclaimed the major, "that the table is not engaged when people are not actually playing!"

The captain answered in a few angry words, when the major, seizing and placing one of the balls before him, vociferated, "I tell you that I have a right to the table, and let me see who will presume to touch this ball."

The captain, without replying, took up a cue, and coolly drove the ball before him. On this, the major struck a violent blow in the face of his antagonist. Several officers rushed forward to interpose, but the captain, anticipating them, addressed the major in something like the following terms: "Sir, you have mortally insulted me, and I shall have satisfaction; but on equal terms, for I shall not allow you to kill me as you boast having done so many others. I hold in my hand a few coins: name you odd or even. If you guess right you will shoot me; but if you miss I shall certainly blow out your brains, for one of us must not leave this room alive."

So saying, he withdrew his closed hand from his pocket, exclaiming, "Now, call out!"

Without appearing much disturbed, the major sung out, "Even!"

The captain then laid his open hand on the table, saying

to the friends of the major, "Gentlemen, be pleased to count." There were seven Napoleons displayed to the view of all.

The captain turned to the friend with whom he had been playing, and desired him aloud to go to his lodging and bring him his pistols, which were loaded. He departed, and the captain locked the door after him, putting the key in his pocket. The persons present, about twenty in number, walked silently about the room, awaiting the sequel of this exciting scene. The messenger returned, handed the pistols to his friend, who forthwith stepped up to the major, and presented the weapon to his face with the words, "Are you ready?"

The two friends of the major now wished to interpose their mediation, which the captain firmly declined to permit; till, finally, on their observing that the major was paymaster to his corps, and had some important papers to settle, it was agreed that he should be allowed to withdraw for the space of half an hour; his friends, meanwhile, remaining as guarantees for his return. This was done, and in the meantime the two gentlemen, renewing their kind endeavours, said almost jocularly: "But surely, captain, you do not intend to avail yourself of your right, and shoot him?"

"But I assuredly do intend it," retorted the captain, "I shall, however, for your sakes, gentlemen, leave him one other alternative, which will be that he will leap out of this window into the street; if he decline to avail himself of this chance, I shall certainly make a hole in him."

Half an hour—a whole hour elapsed—and the Grand Diable had not reappeared. The only information obtained, two or three days later, was that on the day of the above events, he had been seen passing beyond the outposts; thus giving the sad, and I rejoice to add, the solitary instance of a French officer deserting to the enemy; if I except the infamous treason of Bourmont, on the eve of Waterloo.

About the same time a ludicrous incident occurred, which occasioned a good deal of merriment in the army. I relate it as exhibiting the artless and implicit confidence which the soldiers reposed in the emperor's word, and also in his power.

Some depredations having been committed in the country by our troops, Napoleon issued an order of the day, denouncing severe penalties upon the perpetrators of such outrages, and, at the same time, promising that all losses arising from such cases, on being satisfactorily proved, should be paid by the intendant general of the army.

A marching company of infantry had been quartered for the night in a large inn, situated in a suburb of the ancient town of Donauwerth, on the Danube; and the men rejoiced at being assigned as their dormitory an immense barn, filled with hay and other provender. During the night the captain's attention was aroused by a loud altercation which proceeded from the barn, and thither he hastily repaired. He arrived in time to hear the conclusion, which was somewhat as follows: "Oh! mister soldier! in the name of all the saints!" exclaimed in broken French, and in a most dolorous tone of voice, the proprietor of the inn, "I humbly beg you will not go on smoking there; you may set my poor property on fire, and still worse, burn the whole city of Donauwerth!"

"Well!" roared out the soldier, "what of that, you old fool? Have you not read the emperor's order of the day, placarded on all the walls of the town? Why, if I burn it, they'll pay it to you, your old city!"

Napoleon, before the public, thought it desirable to appear stern, even to severity; but, with his friends, such as Cambacérès, Murat, Caulaincourt, Duroc, and Savary, he yielded to his natural affability, and even, sometimes, indulged in a good-natured jest or pleasantry. After the conclusion of the campaign of Wagram, the emperor returned to France. He was met on the bridge of the Rhine by an immense concourse of people, and ft deputation headed by M. de Pontécoulant, prefect of the department of Bas-Rhine, and one of the most eminent among the civilians of this epoch.

The prefect had carefully prepared an address suited to the occasion; but the excitement of the moment, the display of military pomp, the surrounding staff, perhaps also some of that uncontrollable feeling at sight of the emperor which I had myself experienced, and which at this time was shared by nearly the whole of France: all these causes combined produced so powerful an effect on M. de Pontécoulant that he suddenly totally forgot his intended speech. However, in hopes that once the ice was broken, he might recover his treacherous memory, he ventured to begin in tremulous accents: "Sire, your faithful subjects of the city of Strasbourg are so happy at seeing you again that—that—Sire, your faithful subjects are so happy that"—

"Oh! yes!" the the emperor exclaimed, at the same time shaking cordially the dismayed prefect by the hand, "My friend, M de Pontécoulant, and the kind citizens of Strasbourg are so happy to see me that they can not express their joy!"

On one occasion, Savary, the minister of police, gave notice to the emperor of an individual who had repeatedly solicited an audience of his majesty. He had been refused admittance, being an absolute stranger, but he was still, at that moment, sitting on the staircase of the Tuileries. Napoleon desired his immediate admittance, upon which he was introduced by Savary. Napoleon asked the man his business.

"Sire," was the reply, "the communication I have to make is of such a nature that to your majesty alone I can entrust it."

The emperor then desired Savary to leave the room, and resumed his writing. A few minutes passed, and the stranger, remaining silent, Napoleon exclaimed, with some irritation, "Well, why don't you speak?"

"Sire," answered the man, "as I stated before, I can not speak unless to your majesty alone."

The emperor turned around, and seeing Savary still standing near the door of the apartment, reiterated in a stern voice the order to leave the room. Savary hastily answered: "I will not, Sire. This fellow has a villainous physiognomy; and besides, from information I have procured, I find he is a Corsican; I do not trust him."

"Ah! indeed!" said the emperor, with a smile; "a Corsican, is he? Well, so am I. Leave us instantly."

The stranger remained closeted for a considerable time with Napoleon; and conjecture itself has never been able to ascertain who he was or the character of his errand. This incident is more than alluded to in the *Mémoires de Savary*, but not mentioned in the *Mémorial de St. Hélène*. The campaign being ended, we went by short stages through the greater part of Germany, and through a large part of Trance, diagonally, having recrossed the Rhine at Dusseldorf, and scarcely halting for one day, until we reached Bayonne. There we remained four days, to renew our arms and accoutrements, and to receive recruits, having left four hundred of our men buried in German soil. We re-entered Spain on the 6th day of October, 1809, as a part of the corps commanded by Marshal Ney.

Here, what a contrast awaited even those of us who had previously visited Iberia. To the *sauerkraut*, the noodles, and the white beer, which we had abundantly enjoyed in Bavaria, and scantily in Austria, had succeeded, in our passage through France, the usual rations of rather poor meat, *pain de munition, id est,* bread made half of rye flour and half of wheat and bran; the whole seasoned with as much cold water as the men were inclined to imbibe. Still, we were then on our native soil, and the hospitable inhabitants, although already taxed by the incessant passage of numerous armies, exerted themselves to the utmost to evince their sympathy with the men who had fought abroad the battles of the fatherland.

Here in Spain, for food, a solid, massive bread, composed of maize, with a small proportion of wheaten flour; garvanzos, tomatoes, pimentos, a rare distribution of skinny, meager goats' flesh, accompanied by a scanty allowance of tolerably good wine, but so saturated with the taste and odour of the goatskins in which it had been transported that the men at first could scarcely be induced to taste it—such, generally, was the fare that awaited us in Spain—happy, if even this could always be available.

The climate brought us another disappointment. I, like many others, had formerly visited Spain in summer only, and we represented the country as being warm indeed, but heavenly in its generally pure atmosphere, its balmy zephyrs, and its luxuriant, healthy soil. War, it must be remembered, had not at that time devastated the country in which we were, as yet, generally regarded as friends, and we had left it with minds fully disposed to describe couleur de rose everything connected with Spain. We very soon had to admit a strange contrast to our fond anticipations.

In some respects, however, our people were not disappointed; and especially in the language of the country. This so much resembled their own that they were enabled readily to guess, if not fully to comprehend, its meaning; they were aided also by the intelligent, earnest gestures, which were never-failing accompaniments of every word uttered.

The common character of the Spaniards was likewise strikingly agreeable. The long occupation of Spain, combined with native manners derived from their Gothic ancestors, the Moors, then the most civilized people on the globe, and the blind subserviency of the people to the double tyranny of the court and the clergy, had stamped the personality of the middle classes, as well as that of the peasantry and of the working classes, with a submissive cast of deportment, which was by no means indicative of servile submission, but rather of a respectful, though distant regard; for, in their conduct toward their superiors, I have often noticed a certain degree of haughtiness which betrayed an origin of Moorish nobility.

But the temperature of the country very soon led the newcomers to accuse of optimism those of us who had given so flaming an account of the climate. When engaged in the defiles of the Guadarrama, we happened to be overtaken by a furious snowstorm, and that so suddenly that we were not fully prepared for winter. My company was quartered in a small village, the name of which I shall not forget, for there I encountered the severest cold I ever experienced anywhere. It was called Villalba, within a short distance of the famed castle of San Ildefonso, and of La Granza (the barn), the favourite residence of several Spanish monarchs.

It does not enter into the plan of this narrative to attempt topographical descriptions, yet I can not pass on without giving a brief account of a monument which appeared to me as stupendous, regarded as a work of art, as those creations of Divine power, the Falls of Niagara, or the snow-capped dome of Mont Blanc. I allude to the aqueduct, which, after traversing ten miles of hill and vale, supplies San Ildefonso and Segovia with water. This work, unique in its grandeur, has been attributed to Trajan, but the simple natives doubt such an origin, and very generally affirm that the aqueduct has always existed, and was not constructed by human bands. Imagine a structure composed of two stone canals superposed with an interval of some twenty feet, and composed in their whole course of ten miles of enormous blocks of granite, so admirably fitted to each other, that without a particle of cement, not a drop of water can escape, and you may form some conception of the aqueduct of Segovia.

From old Castile we went through Madrid and New Castile to Estremadura; here nothing occurred which could tally with the object of this memoir. However, I may not omit stating an observation which struck us all, and, if well founded, is an anomaly peculiar to Spain, in contradistinction to other nations. In France, in Germany, in England, you may distinguish the natives of the several provinces by some intonations or peculiar patois, hut in general characteristics they are still essentially French, German, English. In Spain you may at once discern perceptible differences, not so much in language as in manner, complexion, and customs.

To the lively, smart manners, the spirited disposition of the Arragonese, to the affected pride of the inhabitants of Madrid, and the wretched misery of the country parts of old Castile, succeeded in Estremadura a listless sort of apathy, a gravity of deportment, which might be ascribed less to physical constitution than to the isolation in which the province was left by the want of roads and other means of communication with foreign countries, or even with neighbouring provinces. Yet the people are reasonably proud, deriving, as I said, this trait from their former rulers, the civilized Moors; and in the midst of poverty to which they seem reconciled, they make excellent soldiers. The best horsemen in the Spanish army are natives of Estremadura.

At Truxillo, I witnessed that darling spectacle of Spaniards, a bull fight. I was disappointed in the expectations raised previously by hearsay or by written accounts, I saw nothing here but wretched panic-struck bulls, maimed or butchered by awkward matadors and two miserable horses gored by the bulls.

At Merida, where we were quartered, we found a town of few inhabitants, but of large extent, and possessing majestic tokens of ancient splendour in the numerous monuments left by the Romans, at the time of their occupation.

Our corps now returned northward to the province of Leon, and there accident occasioned the most active service I had as yet experienced. The head-quarters of our division was at Salamanca. Whilst in that city, I was ordered, with a section of my company, to escort a small convoy to the town of Toro. There, the feeble garrison being deemed insufficient to resist the numerous guerillas with which it was surrounded, I was detained, nolens volens, by the general commanding, and employed during the month of January in hunting for guerillas, generally with little success; they were too nimble and also too well acquainted with the country. There was no question of a regular engagement, but now and then, over hedges or other enclosures, we were suddenly assailed with a volley of musketry, and our only satisfaction was to see a dozen men running full speed in a direction in which it would have been madness to follow. I lost four men in one of these ambuscades.

On my return to Salamanca, I found that my regiment had gone to share in the siege of Ciudad Rodrigo; and again I was detained by General Thirbauch, the chief of the staff, for nearly the same reasons that had caused my detention at Toro; the only difference was, that in addition to chasing the guerillas, and protecting communications on the roads to Toro and Valladolid, I had to levy contributions of provisions and forage through a district of several leagues in extent. According to orders, I always delivered to the people levied upon a receipt, forming a draft on the intendant of the army, hut I can not assert that these drafts were very punctually honoured.

This service was the most agreeable I ever had in the army. In the first instance, I was, when on special duty, general-in-chief of my detachment; obliged to obey orders as to the object of the expedition, but with absolute carte blanche as to the details. Besides, my detachment had been doubled, by receiving into it all men leaving the hospital. From the same source, I received all the accoutrements I wanted. As to food, we took, care of that in the villages that we visited, although we never slept in one for fear of being surprised by guerillas, but uniformly camped out of town. My men carried no money, and thus the guerillas, knowing that no booty was to be obtained from them except the contents of their cartridge-boxes, and this in a manner not altogether pleasant, very seldom attacked us.

Here it strikes me that the reader may justly be surprised that so independent a service as that described above should have been entrusted to the hands of such a youngster as I was. This would at once be understood by those familiar with the French army at that time, but here demands some explanation.

In England, the honour grades of officers, with very few exceptions, are filled up by purchase, and afterwards permit exchanging from one corps to another, with little or no difficulty. In Germany, the sons of nobles, or of persons high in office, alone enjoy the privilege of entering the army as officers; it was so, at least, at the time of which I write. Quite different was the system followed in France. All private soldiers, whose conduct and ability entitled them to this distinction, were recommended by the council of administration of their respective regiments, then approved by the minister of war, and finally nominated by the emperor to the rank of sous-lieutenant (corresponding to the title of ensign in England and to that of second lieutenant in the United States).

A few midshipmen were transferred from the navy to this rank in the army. But by far the greater number of our sous-lieuten-ants had been pupils of the military school at Fontainebleau, and later at Saint Cyr. At the period of this narrative, education was at a very low ebb indeed throughout France, except in the cities, where good schools were well supported. But in the country parts, from which we received nine-tenths of our recruits, the native intelligence of the people rendered less baneful the al-most total absence of literary instruction. Hence, incredible as it may appear, in a company of one hundred and twenty-one men, I have, excluding sergeants and corporals, counted only eight men capable of reading or writing. From this strange state of ignorance arose a curious result, peculiar, I believe, to the French army, and pregnant with remarkable consequences.

The young men in the ranks had, when leaving home, left earnest requests for news to be forwarded to them by letters written by the priest or the school-master of their respective villages. Such letters, after reaching the regiment, had to be read and answered, but by whom? for they sometimes contained in-formation either ludicrous or susceptible of bringing a blush to the cheek of the recipient. To communicate such correspond-ence to those of their comrades learned in the alphabet might have exposed them to the jeers and perhaps the contempt of their fellow soldiers; to apply to field officers, or even to captains, would have been too wide a leap over the chasm separating the ranks; there remained one resource—the sous-lieutenants. These were nearly of an age with the recruits, and sufficiently superior in rank to remove the fear of indiscretion among the soldiers; hence, the sous-lieutenant, or sometimes the first lieutenant of each company, became the amanuensis, and necessarily the inti-mate confidant of the great majority of his men.

It was thus, that before I was twenty years of age, I had become acquainted with the special and family affairs of upwards of fifty men, and had written for them several wills, powers of attorney to their relatives, or vows of eternal love to their sweethearts. The consequences may be anticipated. The young officers be-came seriously interested in the welfare of their men; the latter could hardly find opportunities enough to evince their ardent attachment for their youthful protectors. Many a field officer was left for a time, wounded on the field, for a sous-lieutenant must first be removed out of the fire. In times of scarcity, and we experienced many such, as I may have occasion to state hereafter, I had more than once the satisfaction of sharing with my captain, or the major of the battalion, bread, tobacco, eggs, meat, poultry, rabbits, wine, etc.; the fruits of some successful marauding of my men. The remarkable progress of education within the last fifty years leads me to surmise, that with the cause the effect has vanished, and thus put an end to the system in question.

An incident which occurred in the month of June, 1810, forming rather a prominent event in my army life, I can scarcely omit the mention of it in these reminiscences of my former career.

The band of guerillas commanded by Don Julian Sanchez, in the west, had not an equal in Spain, with the exception of the one in the north, directed by the celebrated Mina. Don Julian had for his most zealous lieutenant a young man, who, for some motive of private revenge, rather than patriotism, had forsaken his profession of lawyer to raise a band of guerillas, whom he dressed in French uniforms; for he was said to have made a vow not to spare the life of any French soldier who should fall into his hands.

One evening I arrived at Salamanca with a supply of provisions, and very tired, after a long march under a midsummer sun. My report being made, I returned to the convent, the great refectory of which was always reserved for my detachment; saw my men all sound asleep on their straw, and lay down myself, rejoicing in the idea of making a night of it. About eleven o'clock my sentry awoke me, introducing an orderly, who brought a command to attend immediately at head-quarters, on the great square of the city. I can not speak very flatteringly of the good grace with which I obeyed this unseasonable infringement of my repose, but obey I must, and did.

General Thiébault was writing at his desk when I made my

appearance, and his first words were: "How many men have you now?"

"Eighty-four, Sir."

"Well," he continued, "you shall start immediately with your whole detachment, and not stop until you reach the village called Los Pavones."

"Sir!" I exclaimed, involuntarily, "Los Pavones is eleven Spanish leagues (about forty English miles) from this, and my men are nearly used up with the last ten days' march in the mountains, and"—

"Enough," said the general, sternly. "Don Aguilar is ill in the priest's house at Los Pavones; the man whom you see there sitting in the corner is a spy, who has already done good service, and who undertakes to conduct you to the very house."

The general need not have said so much; the very name of Aguilar struck through my whole being a chord which would have vibrated in the heart of the most apathetic man in the army. I eagerly undertook the mission, received a few more instructions on the subject, and reflecting that it would be impossible to reach my destination in less than ten hours, and that to attempt the capture in daylight would insure its failure, I took upon myself to let my men continue their sleep a couple of hours more, and at two o'clock started, keeping a strict guard on the spy, who accompanied us.

At four o'clock in the afternoon of the next day, we arrived within two leagues of Los Pavones. A large vineyard appearing at a short distance from the road, I marched my men into it, made them lie down, with strict injunctions not to raise their heads, and upon this welcome recommendation, they were all soon sound asleep.

At dusk, under a gentle shower of rain, we started again, and reached our destination between ten and eleven o'clock. The spy brought us faithfully to the door of the priest's house. Leaving the sergeant to watch in front, I went with a part of my men to place sentinels in a garden which seemed to surround the place.

During my short absence, a servant-girl happened to come out with a pail of water, which she was probably about to empty into the street. My sergeant had the presence of mind to throw his arm around the girl's face, thus effectually preventing any noise on her part. I returned at this moment and the door being half open, I went in, accompanied by a dozen men. On entering the hall, I saw a light issuing from an apartment, the door of which was wide open. To this I proceeded, securing in my hand a pocket pistol, which had been given me by my brother, and which had accompanied me in all my expeditions. Having little doubt of being near the successful issue of the adventure, I plunged at once into the room, and beheld—not Aguilar, indeed, but a venerable old man, sitting up in bed, and reading by the light of a lamp.

At sight of me and my men, he uttered an exclamation of terror, which I soon silenced. After he had somewhat recovered, I learned from him that Aguilar was, indeed, in the house, where he had been compelled to receive him; that he was now in an apartment at the end of the hall, and, as he verily believed, in a dying state. To the room thus indicated, we instantly repaired; the door was locked inside, but three or four stout men soon removed this obstacle.

At this moment, there was a great crash in the room, and two shots fired outside. We rushed in, and saw through the feeble obscurity of a June night, a bed on the right hand side of the room. We threw ourselves precipitately on this bed, and called loudly for a light. I felt no movement under me, but my hair was suddenly grasped most violently, which caused me to undergo intolerable pain.

A light was finally brought in, and showed the singular spectacle of six men overlaying a motionless body, while one of these men, myself, was held most unmercifully by the hair and throat, in the hands of—my own sergeant!

Aguilar had not fainted, although labouring under a heavy

fever, but he was taken by surprise, and rendered absolutely powerless.

The noise we had heard was occasioned by the hasty opening of a window and two shots from my men, by which one of Aguilar's attendants had been killed on the spot; the other escaped. Two loaded pistols were on a table in the middle of the room and two helmets belonging to French dragoons.

We found in the stable a couple of excellent horses fully equipped. After having regaled my men with whatever the house afforded, and taken some hours' rest, we bound Aguilar, placed him in a sort of buggy belonging to the priest, and made the latter mount his mule to accompany us. This proceeding was not accomplished without the most pitiful lamentations from the poor old man; for, by an order of the day, to which the utmost publicity had been given, any person receiving a guerilla into his house was liable to capital punishment. I assured him that I would see him safe from any penalty, but that my orders to bring him with me were imperative.

Our march was uninterrupted by accident, and we reached Salamanca about eight o'clock the next evening. I rode one of the horses we had captured, and during the march used my utmost Spanish eloquence to convey some comfort to the heart of my unhappy prisoner, assuring him that the worst he had to expect was to be sent as a prisoner of war to France, where the best treatment awaited him.

But all my endeavours were vain; either Aguilar did not understand me, or he disdained to answer, but he observed throughout an obstinate and contemptuous silence, and utterly refused to accept any nourishment, with the exception of two glasses of lemonade.

In coming down to see the prisoners, General Thiébault asked for the priest. I pointed to him, where he sat trembling on his mule to the left of the detachment, but told the general that I was certain the old man had acted under compulsion, and that, besides, I had given my word that he should be set at liberty on our arrival.

"You were very wrong to promise such a thing," was the answer, "but it is nearly dark; send him off quietly. I'll not see him." The poor priest did not need much explanation; he testified his satisfaction by plying the flanks of his mule vigorously with his heels, and soon disappeared.

Two days later, my unhappy prisoner was tried by court-martial, convicted by the testimony of some of his own countrymen, of barbarous murders committed upon French soldiers, and hung on the main square of Salamanca. He had to be carried, already half dead, to the place of execution; I did not, could not witness the last scene, though I was present at the trial.

A few days after, I obtained leave to rejoin my regiment at Ciudad Rodrigo, and thence to the short siege of Almeida. The army, which now took the denomination of "Army of Portugal," was commanded by Marshal Masséna, Prince of Essling. It numbered fifty-four thousand men, and reckoned among its chief officers such men as Ney, Junot, Loison, Reille, and other distinguished military characters.

Almeida, after the expolosion of its pricipal magazine, surrendered; an indescisive engagement took place in its vicinity and the English army commenced its retreat towards Lisbon. We soon followed, having first provided each soldier with five days' provisions; for Lord Wellington had issued a proclamation inviting the Portuguese to follow his army, taking away all they could carry, and burnung or destroying the rest.

The inhabitants very generally complied, and thus set an example, which, thre years later, was followed by the Russians at Moscow. Here then we had before us a march of two hundred miles across a mountainous country, nearly deserted by its population, and bare of all kinds of supplies. The men, overloaded with their accroutrements, their arms, their sixty rounds of cartridges and their five days' rations of provisions, soon threw away a part of latter. and we had barely reached Guarda before scarcity began to be sensibly felt.

The enemy continued their retreat making no stand until at Busaco September 27, 1810, the Sixth Corps to which my regiment belonged, found itself ten miles in advance of the fourth corps, with the commander-in-chief, and two miles in advance of the second corps, under the command of General Reille.

The enemy must have been well aware of this faulty disposition; for, instead of continuing their retreat, they had halted at Busaco, and the first thing we perceived, on arriving, was a battery of eight guns frowning on an eminence commanding the village. Marshal Ney, the commander of our corps, came to reconnoitre the position, and with his usual impetuosity, led our regiment to the village, which the English soon abandoned, and then sent us, under General Simon, to storm the battery. We did so, and at first did not meet with any serious rebuff. Suddenly, however, from three sides of the hill, appeared masses of infantry, in numbers sufficient to annihilate our poor 26th Regiment.

In less time than I can describe it, the tide of affairs changed woefully. General Simon was knocked off his horse, with a ball in his neck, and left on the field for dead, our colonel (Barrère, brother of the notorious Jacobin) was killed, as well as three of our majors, eight captains, four lieutenants, and about four hundred rank and file. A panic ensued among us, and contrary to those heroes who boast of never having turned their backs to the enemy, I must confess that on the order to retreat, given by our remaining major (later our excellent colonel, Ferry by name), we did not wait for an additional command of quick step, but showed our discrimination between going up and coming down hill. I, for one, must confess that I never appreciated more fully the good sense of that saying of Napoleon, *"L'art de la guerre est dans les jambes, autant que dans la tête.*[1] Our colours were saved, and a considerable promotion took place in the regiment, now much reduced in numbers, so that we accepted our discomfiture philosophically enough; though bitter reflections were made on the reckless manner in which Marshal Ney had sacrificed our corps. His rash conduct highly incensed the

1. "The art of war is in the legs as much as in the head."

Prince of Essling, and the coolness which had for some time been suspected to exist between the two chiefs soon became apparent to the army.

The southward march of both armies continued, without any other serious conflict, till, reaching the strong position of Torres Vedras, the enemy came to a full stand, and Massena was so struck with the natural strength of the heights that he devoted four days to a careful study of the approaches, and finally concluded on the inexpediency of storming them. Meanwhile, Wellington, profiting by our hesitation, procured from Lisbon a fleet, as well as a vast force of artillery, with which he covered all available points, thus rendering his lines really impregnable. Marshal Ney, who on our arrival, had strongly recommended an immediate attack, had the indiscretion to blame publicly the inopportune delay of his superior, hinting that the latter was no longer the Massena of 1796, and that, had we attacked at once, we might almost with ease, have annihilated the English army. Ney was probably right in his opinion, but his giving vent to it in angry and indiscreet words, sure to be repeated, widened the unhappy breach between the marshals, and had an indirect effect on the issue of the campaign.

Entrenched camps were soon established in various directions; that of our brigade was on the road to Santarem. The rainy season had begun; we had no stores, and no possibility of communication with Spain; food, forage, clothing, all necessaries, even to a sufficiency of ammunition, were woefully scarce, and to prevent starvation, the army was soon reduced to the necessity of marauding. This was carried on by organized parties detached from each regiment, and sent to parts of the country not occupied by either of the belligerents.

Such expeditions, unavoidable as they were, soon proved of little avail, and were actually injurious to discipline. Parties, commanded by captains of companies, frequently returned with very meager supplies, and, in three or four cases, without their commander, who had been assassinated, the men asserted, by the country people. Stringent orders were promulgated, a few examples were made, but to little purpose; the evil continued. At last, at the suggestion, it was said, of General Loison, the command of such parties was entrusted to the young officers. These, less severe than their seniors, and even occasionally winking at unavoidable infringements of orders, very generally returned to camp with abundance of provisions; in several such expeditions under my command, I never discovered that any of my men had been guilty of plunder, except for necessary food.

By a sort of tacit, mutual understanding, an intercourse, almost friendly, had established itself between the two armies, when not in actual conflict. At one particular point, the Tagus made a bend, formed by an island occupied by the English. From its banks, English officers had frequently quite amicable conversations with French officers, on their bank of the river. If a British gunboat, unseen by us, came up the river, notice was given us, and we retreated to war-quarters. General Junot was once wounded by neglecting such friendly warning. In all cases, prisoners were treated by both nations with commendable care and courtesy.

Sometime in February, 1811, my company was at the outposts; our first lieutenant had been out all night in search of provisions, and instead of returning to the camp, found it more convenient to stop first at our post, which happened to be in his way. Among the booty secured by his party was an old bull, an animal so rare as to become the object of unanimous acclamation by our party. Captain Grignon, who commanded us, was so transported with joy, that not willing to leave to another the honour of sacrificing the victim, he snatched a musket from the stand of arms, and hastily fired it into the animal's head. The poor brute, which had not even been tied, made a fearful leap forward, and galloped away, precisely in the direction of an English post, not visible from ours, but which we knew to be within half a mile.

Without much hesitation, the following note was written in pencil, on the back of an envelop, *viz*:

Captain Grignon, 26th of the line, presents compliments

to the officer commanding the English post, and requests that he will return his bull."

(This was certainly not a clear case of extradition, but our jolly captain was no casuist, and did not hesitate.) The laconic message was forthwith entrusted to a corporal and four men, in working undress, without arms, and immediately dispatched. It was then about eight o'clock a. m. Several hours passed without the reappearance of our men, and the captain, being relieved at noon, was obliged to return to camp with the company, though beginning to indulge in sad misgivings in regard to his chivalric confidence in an enemy. On reaching the camp, instead of taking the rest which we badly needed, he and I returned to the outpost to satisfy our anxiety

No news had been received there about our stray men, and a vision of a court-martial began seriously to haunt the mind of the captain. However; about five o'clock p. m., we heard great huzzaing, which proceeded from the side of the English posts; forthwith, although it was almost dark, we saw about fifty red coats accompanying, with vociferous acclamations, our five soldiers, who preceded their enthusiastic escort, and who, drunk as Bacchus, were running tacks from one side of the road to the other, while yet seeming to join lustily in the outbursts of their excited new comrades.

The English stopped as soon as they came within range of our sentries, and returned to their own quarters, after shaking hands heartily with our men. The latter at last reached us, and threw down their load, consisting of sundry pieces of beef, several loaves of bread strung on a rope, and two skins full of wine. As to explanations, we found it vain to extract any from them. They could utter nothing but drunken shouts to the honour and glory of the English, who had treated them like princes, in the way of drink especially. We were forced to leave them at the post, to sober themselves by sleep. It was not until .the next day that the corporal bethought himself of presenting to the captain a note addressed to him, together with two or three English newspapers which he had the day before carefully concealed under his clothes. The note, written in tolerably correct French, ran in something like the following terms:

> Major ——, of the —— regiment, presents his compliments to Captain Grignon, and regrets to have only a part of the bull to return, beef being a scarce article in his quarters. As a compensation, he begs acceptance of a few loaves of bread and a little wine.

I was soon called upon to translate (a task I could better perform than that of conversing), such passages of the paper as referred to our army, or to the emperor, under such titles as Bony, Nap, Nappy, or similar abbreviations, by which, in these papers, he was uniformly designated. We were soon horrified by the degrading, and to us blasphemous epithets unsparingly attached to the name and character of our demi-god, and I found the greatest difficulty in softening expressions which I shuddered to translate. We were not at the end of our troubles. In the evening of this same day, Captain Grignon was summoned before the commander-in-chief, made to relate all the circumstances of the transaction, and was finally dismissed with a sound reprimand and a severe admonition for the future. The next day, an order of the day was read before all the corps of the army, denouncing severe penalties against any one guilty of receiving communications of any sort from the enemy, and of introducing such into our camps.

At last, the time came when we were obliged to retire with as good a grace as we could assume. The country, for twenty miles round, was thoroughly depleted of all resources; many of our men were dressed like Harlequins, and in one regiment (my own) 850 men had, not bad shoes only, but no shoes at all. The only things of which we had a sufficiency was tobacco, a store of, this article having been somewhere unearthed, and many, many a meal was taken on smoke! The scarcity of ammunition was also a source of uneasiness at head-quarters.

Our retreat began about the 10th of March, 1811. The English army had, meanwhile received considerable reinforcements from England, besides the thousands of volunteers levied in Portugal; but it was abundantly supplied with all requisites, whilst, as I said above, we were in a state of almost absolute destitution. However, as we showed a bold front, and had repulsed several outpost skirmishes, we were not seriously molested, except on three occasions. The first was at Liria. This town boasted of only one wide street, through which our army had to continue its retreat. The enemy pressed closely on our rear with a powerful artillery, while ours was already far beyond Liria. There was but one resource left us. Orders were given to the last column, and as they left the above-mentioned street, they set fire to both sides of it, and the enemy had the mortification of seeing us quietly reach the position previously appointed.

At the passage of the Mondego, a circumstance occurred similar to one more disastrous that happened at Leipsic, three years later. A sergeant of artillery, who had been left at the bridge with orders to blow it up after all the retreating army had crossed, became so confused 'that he set fire to the mine when a considerable number of men were still on the enemy's side of the river. At Leipsic, the unhappy blunder caused the death of a hero, Prince Patowsky, and the capture of several thousand men. On the Mondego, a part of the Thirty-Sixth Regiment was cut off, and a whole convoy of mules abandoned to the enemy.

At Sabugal, near the frontier of Spain, we had a smart engagement, as if to bid a cordial farewell to our British escort; and, to our great satisfaction, we re-entered Spain, where we found comparative abundance of supplies, and, what was not to be despised, ten months' pay, then due us.

We had hardly reached Salamanca when information was received that Lord Wellington had invested Almeida, our last hold on Portugal. Back again we had to go by forced marches, and once more confronted the enemy on the third of May, 1811, at a village called Fuentes D'onores, in the vicinity of Almeida. This was a memorable day for me, as it influenced all my subsequent life by arresting my fond aspirations after promotion in a military career.

I was, during the greater part of the day, engaged *en tirailleurs*, and at night was placed with forty men at an out-post. During the night General Loyson came to the post, accompanied by a single aid. He ordered me to take out twenty men, and to lead him in the direction which I thought likely to discover the nearest English posts. We went on stealthily for about half an hour, when the general told me that I was probably mistaken in my surmises, and that he was going to return to the camp. He, however, desired me to proceed for some time further, instructing me in case I should be challenged or fired at by a foreign vedette, not to answer, but to run back with my men to our post, and send word to head-quarters.

The night was very dark, and a drizzling rain was falling; our silent march was now on a narrow road, flanked by a hedge on either side. The general had not left us ten minutes when, on reaching an opening of the road, a perfect avalanche of blows overwhelmed my unlucky party in about the space of one minute. Not a shot was fired, the bayonet and the butt ends of muskets alone did the work, and strange to say, although all were more or less wounded, only one man, who had formerly been a drummer, was killed outright. As for myself, before I could well guess into what a wasp's nest I had fallen I was laid prostrated by a blow on the head, and with a slight bayonet or sword wound in my left shoulder. When I recovered my senses, for I had fainted, I found myself lying on the grass, and surrounded by red coats.

A gentleman, whom I afterwards learned was Sir Charles Stewart, addressed me in excellent French, and in very soothing terms. Soon a surgeon made his appearance, and declared that the worst harm had been the blow on the head, and that a few days would see me well. I then learned that I had fallen into a post composed of two whole companies; that my advance had been detected several minutes before the onset; and I was thankful that General Loyson had been so well inspired as to part with me when he did. Being sent to the rear, I met in the hospital, at Celorico, an officer whom the day before I had observed falling from our desultory fire; he had received a ball in his knee, from which resulted permanent lameness; his acquaintance became valuable to me later on. His name was A. H. Pattison, of Glasgow, and he was, I believe, a captain in the 74th Regiment.

At Lisbon, where I arrived a few days later, I had an unexpected and agreeable meeting. As we, prisoners of war, escorted by a detachment of infantry, were about to enter Fort Belleim, our destination until our embarkation for England, we met a number of English officers loitering near the gate of the fort. One of them approaching us suddenly gazed at the number on my shako, then on the buttons of my uniform, and thereupon called out excitedly to his comrades, who soon crowded round us. It turned out that these gentleman were officers of the 26th Regiment, British infantry, which formed at this time the garrison of Fort Belleim. They asked and obtained leave to keep me in their quarters during my detention there, and commenced their kind acts of hospitality by making me, at their mess, gloriously forgetful of my captivity, and of all other ills of this nether planet.

A few days of this mode of life, altogether new to me, soon proved prejudicial to my health, and the regimental doctor declared that a continuation of such diet would soon consign me to Portuguese soil. The fact was, that the weather being very hot, the unaccustomed potations and high living began to tell seriously on the wound in my shoulder, and I had once more to be an inmate of the hospital. Here I met again my quondam friend, Captain Pattison, who, although much more grievously wounded than myself, yet contrived to show me every attention in his power. Not the least of these was to obtain for me a berth on the ship in which he returned to England, instead of in one specially allotted to prisoners of war. I was then quite recovered in health, and had a very pleasant voyage of ten days to Portsmouth. I fared well on the passage, a quantity of delicacies having been sent on board for me by my over-hospitable entertainers of the 26th Regiment.

All the prisoners, numbering about sixty, were landed at Gosport, a small town situated on the western side of the bay, opposite Portsmouth, and in which was established the principal depôt of French soldiers, prisoners of war. Here, an unexpected pleasure awaited me. Nearly two years previously I had persuaded my nurse, who lived in a village ten leagues from Paris, to allow one of her sons, my foster-brother, to enlist into my own regiment. The conscription was sure to overtake him before many months, and he would probably be assigned to a regiment, in which, having no friends, his life would not be a very easy one. He joined our corps, and at my request, was attached to my company. Proving to be a very intelligent cheerful young man, he soon became a favourite both with officers and men, and, being a sort of model soldier, had every prospect of rising in his profession. On the evening of the battle of Busaco, at roll call, I was dismayed beyond expression at his not answering to his name. I had seen and spoken to him several times during the day, but, in the confusion that followed, I had lost sight of him. The painful task of announcing his probable death to his mother devolved upon me; I, however, expressed a faint hope of his having been taken prisoner.

We, the officers, were quartered temporarily in a separate building, and were allowed, on our parole, to walk about the town. Our first impulse was to go and look at and converse with our countrymen, many of whom had already been for years in captivity. Here truth and justice compel me to combat an erroneous belief in regard to the harsh treatment of prisoners of war, which was propagated with a purpose at the time, and upheld by those of our men who were so unfortunate as to be confined in the pontons—*id est*, vessels out of commission, at anchor in the roads. There, indeed, they had a hard fate to bear: wretched food, little exercise extremely strict and occasionally cruel discipline—such was their lot; but we ascertained that none were sent to the pontons but refractory and incorrigible disturbers of the peace at Gosport prison; and also the crews of privateers indiscriminately, as the British government deemed such as having been captured in an illegal mode of warfare.

Whilst walking round the wooden palisade (a *clair-voie* surrounding the vast prison, which contained then upwards of five thousand men, guarded outside by two regiments of militia) I was suddenly startled by a loud exclamation of: "*Mon* lieutenant! *Mon* lieutenant!"

Those who were with me turned round hastily, when the same voice reiterated: "*Mon* lieutenant!" adding my name. I have seldom experienced more exquisite joy than I did then on recognizing my foster-brother, looking well and hearty. After shaking hands cordially with him through the trellis, I called on the commander of the prison, and, stating my case, solicited and obtained leave to spend the day inside the prison. A prison it was in reality, but resembling in all respects a huge collection of barracks where an admirable organization had been established, with strict yet humane regulations. Here, no moans of despair were heard, no despondent looks observable on the countenances of the inmates, but on all sides resounded shouts of laughter, or snatches of patriotic songs. This philosophical making the best of things might in part no doubt have been attributed to the happy disposition of my countrymen—long may they cherish it!

I was led by my foster-brother to a snug little corner occupied by himself and a comrade, containing an apparently good bed, and other small articles of furniture, partly purchased with their own money. The next compartment was a kitchen, common to two hundred men, and from which exhaled odours not in the least indicative of a famished population. I remained to dinner. I shall not say that the repast was sumptuous, but it was abundantly supplied with good food; and, although served on pewter plates and dishes, with knives and forks to match, it was seasoned with such cordial hospitality that the remembrance of that dinner has ever left a pleasant impression on my memory. Wine or alcoholic liquors were not produced, such articles being excluded from the prison; yet we were not restricted to cold water, for we had a sufficiency of such excellent ale as is manufactured in England alone.

Amazed as I was at this display of comfort in such a place, one of my first questions was respecting the source of a degree of opulence for which I could not account. This is the information which I received from my host. He was the son of a basket maker, and himself knew something of the business. On arriving at the prison he availed himself of the permission, liberally given to prisoners, to work at such trades as they might be familiar with, and to sell the produce. Customers were numerous, owing to the cheapness and to the general good quality of the prisoners' work.

This trade, however, had to be abandoned, from the extreme difficulty of procuring material. But straw, in sufficient quantities, was furnished to our men for bedding. Germain L——, after receiving instructions from his fellow-captives, turned his ingenuity to the manufacture of straw hats and bonnets, and soon realized more money than his father could earn at homo. But, alas! this prosperity was of short duration. The straw hat and bonnet manufacters of Portsmouth, and some even of London and Barnstable, joined in an earnest petition to the Transport Board,[2] for the purpose of putting an end to a traffic which very seriously affected their interest.

A total prohibition of such manufacture was, in consequence, issued in the prison. Germain was not discouraged. He soon learned another trade by forming a partnership with one already skilled in the business; this was the manufacturing bones into work-boxes, combs, various kinds of toys, but especially boats and ships. Material was abundant; a sort of market was held twice a week, at which the different messes in the prison sent all the bone they could collect; and a smart competition among the manufacturers gave rather a high value to these bones. My foster brother showed me a frigate, fully rigged, upon which he was then at work, which cost him and his partner six months' assiduous labour, and for which, I was afterwards informed, they

2. The Transport Board was a government commission, to which the care and control of the prisoners of war had been delegated. Its principal agents were officers in the British navy.

obtained the handsome sum of forty pounds sterling ($200). The cordage and sails were constructed of human hair, collected in the prison.

When he was liberated, at the peace in 1814, he carried back to France about one hundred and thirty pounds ($650), the fruit of his industry. Here he bought a small farm, married, and was much esteemed among the inhabitants of his district. Poor rich man! He died of the cholera in 1832. In his conversation he never alluded to the period of his captivity, without expatiating in glowing terms on the integrity and liberality evinced towards him by all the English, with whom he had dealings. Such reports, and many similar ones, circulated through France, tended to weaken the keen feeling of hatred and antagonism, to which war had given rise between the two nations.

I have dwelt, perhaps, too long on this episode of my life, as it may possibly be devoid of interest to my readers; it was far otherwise with me, and I felt almost compelled to consign here this tribute of affection to the memory of my foster-brother, Germain Lamy. Repaying abundantly to me, whilst in captivity, any little services which it had been in my power to render him when with the regiment, could I not justly apply in this case the encouraging exhortation of Holy Writ, "Cast thy bread upon the waters, for thou shalt find it after many days?"

After a few days' stay at Gosport, I was, along with several others transferred, on parole to Odiham, a small town in Hampshire; there nothing occurred worth recording. The number of prisoners-of-war having been, about this period, considerably augmented by the taking of the Isle of France, Martinique, and Guadaloupe, the towns appointed to receive officers on parole in England proper, were found to be so inconveniently crowded that the government decided to quarter a portion of our number in Scotland, where none had-hitherto been sent. (Political reasons precluded Ireland from having any share in the distribution of prisoners.)

Odiham furnished its contingent, and I was one of the party thus transported to Caledonia, where we landed at Leith, on the

1st of October, 1811. From Edinburgh we started for our destination, Selkirk, the county town of Selkirkshire, thirty-six miles south of Edinburgh. On the way, we halted a few hours at Penay, where about two thousand of our soldiers and sailors were confined: the organization and regulations of the prison appeared to us modelled on those we had admired at Gosport.

Selkirk is situated on the river Ettrick, which flows from the west and empties itself into the Tweed, about half a mile from the town. Few of its houses were covered with slate; thatch being predominant. Its population amounted to about two thousand inhabitants, and although previous notice had been given, we found, at first, some difficulty in procuring lodgings for the hundred and ninety men that constituted the new colony. Matters soon altered in this respect; the people of the town found presently that we were cash customers, and they vied with each other in obtaining among us occupants for such of their apartments as they could dispose of.

Pleasant hills encircled the town on all sides; a pretty large square and a fountain occupied its centre; a fine bridge spanned the Ettrick. A plain edifice belonging to the Church of England, and a much larger one owned by the Presbyterians, or rather a sect denominated "Anti-burghers," of whom a venerable, excellent man, named Laroun, was the pastor, were the only buildings worthy of notice in Selkirk.

Our pecuniary means were not ample, but were sufficient, every thing being remarkably cheap as compared with England. Our pay for all ranks, indiscriminately, was half a guinea (about three dollars) a week, regularly paid by the agent every Saturday morning. Besides, the majority of us received more or less money from France, through Th. Coutts, the London banker, who had been selected for this purpose by both governments. One of our number, named Belleville, was wealthy, and received annually about £1,000. My allowance from my family, paid quarterly, was £50.

Altogether, we spent weekly about £150, so that when peace took place in 1814, that is, in the course of two years and a half, we had expended no less a sum that over £4,000, which was quite a consideration in such a small town, without trade or manufactures. In regard to our lodgings, we each paid, on an average, sixty cents a week; we generally clubbed together in a mess of from two to six members. Some of us became very fond of fishing, and successful in the pursuit, the Ettrick and Tweed abounding in trout and eels of excellent quality, as well as a lake in a neighbouring mountain in very delicate pike. We were never molested in this sport, which proved a valuable resource in our culinary establishments.

We were too truly French to allow of our feelings being so utterly depressed by our captivity and the uncertainty of our relief as to make us pine away in useless sorrow or lamentations. A person captured at Martinique succeeded in passing himself off as a naval officer, and was accordingly admitted to his parole; he was one of our Selkirk colony, and possessing some pecuniary means, he procured from Edinburgh a billiard table, and all the requisites for establishing a very good coffee-house, to which no admittance was granted, except to our nationality. Soon after, ascertaining that some of us had received musical instruction, we rented instruments from the capital, and mustered twenty-two efficient performers, who, under the leadership of a very superior violinist, constituted an orchestra superior to any that had ever resounded among the echoes of our Scottish residence. We invited to our concerts, gratuitously, of course, some of the inhabitants with whom we had become acquainted.

These recreations did not long satisfy our native activity. We collected among ourselves a sum of £100, rented a barn in the town, purchased a considerable quantity of lumber, as also necessary tools, and proceeded to construct a theatre, etc.; and also benches sufficient for the accommodation of. two hundred spectators. The orchestra was supplied by our band, already alluded to. The costumes, especially those for female characters, puzzled our ingenuity not a little; none of us had ever been a practical carpenter, upholsterer, tailor, or—apprentice to a dressmaker. Intelligence, however, stimulated by will, may perform small miracles. After several careful rehearsals, we had a select repertory drawn from our most popular tragic or comic authors, besides the partly musical works of our best Vaudevillists. Every Wednesday we had a representation, to which we gave the same invitations as for the concerts on Saturdays, and our barn was usually crowded, though mostly with our own people.

On each of the four roads that converged into the town, and at the distance of one mile, a stone post was planted, and on it was painted the words: "Limit of the prisoners of war." A wag among us rooted up one of these stones, carried and transplanted it a mile further, to the amusement of the town's people, who, to their credit be it told, never in one instance availed themselves of a regulation in virtue of which any person who could swear that he had seen any of us beyond the appointed limit was entitled to receive from the culprit one guinea as a fine. I have repeatedly gone fishing several miles down the Tweed, without ever being fined, or in any way molested.

We had no society in the town, for before our arrival, the few persons who might claim rank as the gentry of the place had, as we understood later, concluded at a meeting held for the purpose, that they would not admit any of us into their circle. We were perfectly independent of their hospitality, and sneered at the absence of it. Advances, however, were made by some of the canny Scotch people in favour of Belleville, whose name I have already mentioned; the reason of this preference, of which he invariably declined to avail himself, was his being known to be very wealthy.

However, we made a few pleasant acquaintances in the vicinity. Few of us will have forgotten the kind attentions which we received from Mr. Anderson, a gentleman farmer, who never seemed more pleased than when he could allure to and entertain in his home those of us who were enjoying the sport of fishing in the river on the banks of which stood his residence. Another friend of ours was a wealthy, retired lawyer, a bon vivant in the full sense of the term, and whose only fault, in our estimation, was his manifest chagrin when we did not keep pace with himself in the copious libations with which he regaled us. A third kind friend was a Mr. Thorburn, also a gentleman farmer, a most cordial host, who seemed bent on making his French guests acquainted with such Scottish delicacies as a grilled sheep's head, haggis, hodge-podge, and a splendid kind of cheese, of his own manufacture.

But there was one person whom I met at this time, the honour of whose acquaintance I did not then appreciate as I should have done in later years. Sir Walter Scott was then plain Mr. Scott, no one, except perhaps his publishers, even suspecting him to be "The Great Unknown," author of Waverly. As to us, we saw in Mr. Scott only the sheriff of Selkirkshire, and a lawyer of some repute in Edinburgh. In the former capacity, he frequently visited Selkirk, when at home at his residence at Melrose Abbey, about three miles distant from us.

Mr. Scott became acquainted with one of our number, named Tarnier, a young man of great talent, excellent education, and remarkable gaiety of disposition. Soon, without the supposed knowledge of the government agent, or rather with his tacit approbation, Tarnier was invited to Melrose Abbey, and gave us grand accounts of his reception there. Presently, and probably at the suggestion of our compatriot, he was authorized by Mr. Scott to bring with him three of his friends at each invitation to dinner at Melrose. Thus I was present on two or three occasions, invited, not by the host himself, but by my friend Tarnier.

The period of the year was, to the best of my remembrance, about February, 1813, and our mode of proceeding was something like the following: Towards dusk, we, the guests, repaired to the mile-stone already mentioned; there a carriage awaited us, and soon conducted us to Melrose Abbey, where we were politely greeted by our host. We only saw Mrs. Scott for the few moments which intervened before dinner was announced, as she was not present at the repast. Mrs. Scott was, we understood, either a native of France, or of French parentage; at least, she spoke our language perfectly; Mr. Scott had married her at Berlin. Our host appeared to us in quite a different light from what we had seen of him in the streets of Selkirk. There, he impressed us as having a good-humoured, rather coarse and unmeaning physiognomy, and awkward, almost vulgar walk and attitudes; this last, perhaps, owing to his lameness.

At Melrose Abbey, we found him a cordial, cheerful gentleman, delicate in his kind attentions to his guests. The apartments were roomy and well-lighted, and the table, if not sumptuously, was at least elegantly, furnished. It need not be expected that I shall give here an elaborate description of the surroundings of the mansion; on both occasions of my visits, we arrived in the dusky twilight, and departed amidst the dark shades of night, by the same conveyance that had brought us.

Thus, with the exception of the dining-room, and a glimpse of the parlour, all I know of Melrose Abbey I have derived from descriptive publications, which any one may read. Neither can it be expected that I shall give any detail of repasts of which I partook some sixty-five years ago. But the general tenor of the conversation is fixed immutably in my remembrance. Our leading topic was not general politics, but minute details connected with the French army, and above all, traits and anecdotes respecting Napoleon seemed to have an absorbing interest for our host, who, we remarked, incessantly contrived to lead back the conversation to the subject, if it happened to have diverged from it. As may be imagined, we took care to say nothing unfavourable to the character and honour of our beloved emperor. Little did we suspect that our host was then preparing a work, published ten years later, under the title of *A Life of Napoleon Bonaparte.*

In this unfair production, which is a stain on the name of its otherwise illustrious author, Sir Walter Scott relates anecdotes and circumstances connected with the emperor, many of which were communicated to him by us, but taking care to accompany each recital with sarcastic innuendoes, and self-invented motives of action, derogatory to the honour of Napoleon. The following is an instance:

During the armistice that followed the battle of Zurich,

Prince Souvaroff and General Massena spent several days in cordial and even familiar conversation in the Italian language. On one such occasion, the Russian general, alluding to certain confiscations of objects of art which had been sent to France, concluded by saying, "*Tutti Francesi sono ladroui!*"

"Oh!" exclaimed Masséna, "tutti??"

"*Tutti no, forse,*" replied Souvaroff, smiling, "*tutti no, ma buona parti.*"[3]—(Bonaparte.)

This witticism, singular indeed as coming from a man known for the rude sternness of his character, and related to Sir Walter by one of us at his table, was seized upon by him as an occasion to avail himself of an authority so great as that of the renowned Russian general, in order to vilify Napoleon by representing him as an insatiable robber; whereas it is notorious that all the objects of art which he took from foreign countries, and especially from Italy, were previously estimated as to their value by a committee composed partly of Italians, and received, not stolen, in lieu of payment of the war indemnities levied on the country. Moreover, it is admitted on all hands, that Napoleon, conveying these treasures to France, never allowed any of them to be placed in his residences as his own private property, but invariably distributed them among the National Museums of Paris and other cities.

Thus passed and ended my brief acquaintance with an illustrious character.

Our friendly intercourse with the worthy inhabitants of Selkirk was interrupted only on two occasions, rather amusing than serious, but which might have become tragical.

On the 15th of August, 1813, we met at a banquet, intended as a celebration of the emperor's birthday. Our coffee-room was the place of meeting; it was on the ground-floor, with windows opening on the public square, and at the outside comer of the building was a narrow lane leading to the rear of the town. About one hundred of us were present, although we had provided for double that number.

---

3. "All Frenchmen are robbers." "Oh! all?" "All no, but a good part."—(Bonaparte.)

The dinner passed off very pleasantly, and after numerous toasts had been disposed of, accompanied by songs, speeches, and acclamations, it was observed that the table still remained loaded with a large quantity of eatables, which we could not consume. It was suggested that the proper use to be made of these good things was to distribute them among the populace, who, by this time, had collected in crowds on the square. To this suggestion, which was unanimously approved, was added another, which was carried by acclamation; this amendment consisted in our requiring that each applicant for our bounty should, previous to his receiving it, take off his hat and shout, "*Vive l'Empereur Napoleon!*"

Accordingly, several of us posted ourselves at the entrance of the lane before mentioned, bearing in one hand half a ham, turkey, or roast beef, etc., and in the other a tumblerful of wine, brandy, or whisky. The difficulty was to induce our pseudo guests to comply with our *sine qua non* condition; all hesitated and held back. Finally, we perceived among the crowd a man who served us as a kind of factotum, and who, in this capacity, made a great deal of money by us. This person, whose real name I never knew, had been nicknamed Bang-bay, from the following circumstances: constantly tormented by simultaneous calls for his services, his usual impatient reply was, By-and-by. This expression, not understood by most of us, was changed into Bang-bay, which was the nearest approach we could make towards pronouncing it, and he was always known amongst us by that euphonious appellation.

As having therefore some authority over this man, we called upon him to come forward; he obeyed, and, after a short hesitation, complied with our condition, received nearly a whole roast turkey, quaffed a brimful tumbler of liquor, and was then dismissed, not back to the square, but through the lane to the rear of the town. From that moment our only difficulty lay in supplying the numbers who pressed forward as candidates for drinking the glorious toast. Soon our supplies gave out, and the loudly expressed dissatisfaction of those who had hitherto only been spectators of the fun gave us infinite satisfaction. It was not to be of long duration. The crowd had slowly dispersed, but half an hour later they again assembled in the square.

We had resumed our seats, and were listening to a song composed for the occasion, when a stone, thrown through the window, struck a captain of artillery named Gruffand. Instantly he sprang out of the window, and addressing the mob in imperious tones, demanded, "What rascal among you threw that stone?"

All kept silent; but seeing a sneer on the countenance of one of the mob, he continued, "Perhaps you did; you who are making faces over there?"

"Perhaps I did," answered the young man boldly.

Hardly had he uttered the words, when Gruffand hurled the stone right in his face, wounding him severely. A tumult was about to ensue, when our attention being drawn to the scene, we seized knives and forks, broke a few chairs to serve us as staves, and sallied forth through the doors and windows, to the rescue of our friend. The people being unarmed, thought it best not to test our weapons, but at once deserted the square. A little later, however, the agent, Mr. Robert Henderson, came hurriedly to give us notice that a new mob was organizing with arms, and that the matter might become very serious; that, moreover, we were in one respect in the wrong, as it was now ten o'clock, whereas by the regulations which we had engaged implicitly to obey, we should have been in our respective lodgings by nine o'clock. e admitted at once the reasonableness of these observations, and retired without molestation. The affair had no sequel, and both parties shortly resumed better feelings towards each other.

Soon, however, we conceived we had another and more serious cause of displeasure. Upon the announcement of a victory of Wellington in Spain, the people of Selkirk had the bad taste, if not the indelicacy, considering our position, to ring all the bells in the town, and to display an extravagant and insulting joy. We were not long in retaliating. Not many days had passed when, one Saturday, news arrived of a great victory gained by the

French army in Russia. Our plans were soon arranged. The following day being Sunday, two of our party attended the service at the meeting house, and they contrived to secrete themselves in such a manner that the doors were closed on them without them being discovered.

At midnight the watchers unbolted one of the windows, and admitted half a dozen of their confederates; these last had provided themselves with a long rope, which was soon fastened to the one attached to the bell. Six stout arms soon developed all its sounding notes, to the imminent danger of cracking the instrument, and, in a few minutes, wonder and consternation spread through the town. Before the crowd, which ran from all quarters, had collected at the church, our party had escaped to their quarters, secure from fear of discovery. Although suspicion strongly pointed our way, nothing could be proved against us, and the affair was dropped.

At last peace was proclaimed, and we were notified that a vessel would be ready at Berwick, on the 26th of April, 1814, to convey us to Boulogne or Calais. I need hardly say with what transports of joy this news was received by us; a joy which I suspect was not shared by those whose lodgings were now to be left vacant.

The few of us who had sufficient pecuniary means proposed to go in carriages to Berwick; hut at a general meeting convened for the purpose, it was proposed by Belleville that all the money we possessed should be merged into one common fund, and distributed equally per capita, so that all should go on the same footing; he himself gave the example by contributing all he had on hand, about £30. The whole sum thus collected not amounting to more than about £60, we concluded that we should all take the journey together, and on foot; one old colonel, and two other officers in ill health, were alone exempted from this arrangement, and a carriage was provided for them.

We had one anxiety in leaving Selkirk, namely, the fear of departing without enjoying another bit of fun; an opportunity, however, presented itself, and we were not disposed to reject it.

The materials for our theatre, consisting of boards, seats, decorations, costumes, etc., had cost us about £120; the work itself cost us nothing, we being our own carpenters, smiths, painters, tailors, etc. These materials would, in our estimation, .provide us with the means of performing our journey more comfortably. Accordingly, we announced that the next day we should sell said lumber, etc., by auction at our barn; one witty young officer, Tarnier, who spoke English fluently, was to act as auctioneer.

At the time appointed, the attendance was large, and looked very encouraging. The starting price was announced to be £50, but soon had to be reduced to £20. From this point, amidst the expostulations of the auctioneer, answered by sneers from a part of the audience, the highest bid offered amounted to £4! We soon had an understanding among ourselves. Our worthy auctioneer announced to the assembly that the barn being too confined, we should proceed with the auction in a field contiguous to the town, and hitherto rented by us for football exercise.

With promptitude, and accompanied by the noisy merriment of the crowd, we shouldered boards, benches, etc., and conveyed them to the new scene of operation. But so careful were we of our neat decorations, scenery, and costumes, that we first laid under them a quantity of straw, and then surmounted the whole with a high pile of lumber. The auction was now resumed, and Tarnier's voluble eloquence was exerted to the utmost to strike any chord of liberality that might slacken a little the purse strings of our Scottish friends. All in vain; the latter knew that the things must be sold, and the highest obtainable bid was £6. A few of us, well provided with steel, flints, and amadon (tinder), were posted round the mass of inflammable material; at a preconcerted signal from our auctioneer, the pile burst into a blaze, to the great danger of setting fire to the town, had there been a wind. The bonfire was greeted by us with hearty shouts of "*Vive l'Empereur*," although we knew that he had already abdicated, and by mingled cries of disappointment and merriment from the crowd of astonished bystanders.

At last the day of our final departure arrived; Tuesday morning was the time appointed. Most of us had passed the night on the square, singing and merry-making, so we were all ready, and were about starting, when a new and pleasant sight met our view. Vehicles of all descriptions were seen pouring down the two principal streets leading to the town—carriages, gigs, wagons, and a few saddle horses; these had been sent by the inhabitants of the neighbourhood to convey us free of expense as far as Kelso, about half way to Berwick. This liberal attention was so well timed and so delicately performed that we could not do otherwise than avail ourselves of it with many thanks, and thus we parted from our Kelso friends without entertaining, on either side, any remnant of grudge that might previously have existed between us.

On arriving at Boulogne, our feelings were sorely tried at perceiving our beloved tricolour replaced on all public buildings by the hated white flag; this unpleasant sensation was intensified a little later by an outrage which aroused all our ill-disposed sentiments.

We had landed about ten o'clock in the morning, and had been directed to the mayor's office, where we were to receive our lodging billets. At four in the afternoon we were still standing or sitting on the pavement in the street awaiting the convenience of his honour, the mayor, a recently returned emigrant. Unfortunately for myself, I happened to be near the office door when it finally opened, and no sooner had I passed the threshold than I poured forth a torrent of indignant reproach on the mayor, and, among other sarcasms, told him that under the emperor he dared not have conducted himself thus shamefully towards French officers returning from captivity. The altercation was cut short by the interference of some of my more cautious friends, but we observed that the mayor took notes, as we rightly conjectured, of my name, and the number of my regiment.

A few days later, I arrived at Paris, and proceeded to the war office to take further orders, first handing, as usual, my card to the usher. Many others were before me, probably on the same errand; but when at last my name was called, I was introduced into the private office of an elderly officer, wearing the uniform of a general. Before I had time to state my case, he asked me when and where I had landed from England; on my answer, he addressed me without hesitation, not a warning—that should have been sufficient, in consideration of my youth, and the position I held—but a severe reprimand, which he concluded by desiring me to leave my address in the lower office. I left in a high state of indignation. Once at home, my first care, in spite of all the entreaties of my friends, was to write in the curtest terms my resignation, and to carry it immediately myself to the war office. By evening of the same day I received the answer, "Your resignation is accepted."

Thus ended, for that time at least, my experience of life in the army.

Voices of 1812

Accounts of Napoleon's
French Soldiers from
the Russian Campaign

Arthur Chuquet

Contents

The Paymaster Duverger

1

In 1812 a young Parisian of eighteen, B. J. Duverger, had just finished his course of study at the Lycée Napoleon. He had a wish to travel, like the greater number of the friends and companions of his youth who had become soldiers and, as he expressed it, were laying up a store of glory.

The first army corps Davout was mustering at Hamburg was growing into an army and appeared to be the vanguard of a formidable expedition.

Where was this mass of fighting men bound for?

Turkey, to deprive the Sultan of his possessions in Europe and Asia? To the Indies, to drive out the English? Or was it to invade Russia, the ally of France? Rumours of rupture were already current; the Tsar was accused of bad faith; he was reproached with being disloyal to the Continental blockade.

But what did it matter to Duverger?

All he wanted was to be up and doing; to see, as said Horace, whom he had been lately translating, the customs and the cities of men.

Provided with letters of recommendation, he went to Hamburg, and obtained a post as paymaster in Campans's division.[1]

2

It was in this way that he followed the Grand Army to Rus-

---

1. See his *Souvenirs* in the *Magazine Français* of December, 1833, pp. 163-189,

sia.

In the early days of June he was on the banks of the Niemen and beginning to know something of the discomforts of war.

Hitherto he had been surrounded by comfort; now he had to bivouac, sleeping in the open air, sometimes on straw, when he could find it, sometimes on the bare ground, and faring meagrely. Where now were the quarters of France and Germany? Where were the little amenities of the paternal roof and his soft bed and abundant table?

Duverger had to put up with it all.

When he crossed the Niemen with the advance guard he does not seem to have suffered from the storm described by Ségur; he heard no claps of thunder, he did not see the heavens discharge their cataracts of rain.

What he recalls was the look of the mounted grenadiers of the Guard in the evening: their long white cloaks; their enormous bearskins; their big black horses they held by the bridle; the silence that reigned in their ranks; all this made a profound impression on the young man's mind; all this, he says—and in this part of his account can be traced the influence of Ossian—all this called up before his eyes the fantastic pictures in the poetry of the bards of the North.

The next day he received another impression—a disquieting and alarming impression, which he describes with a very good grace. He lost his way and strayed about in an immense wood. For two hours he rode about without meeting a soul, and, little by little, all his stock of martial and heroic sentiments faded away. His love of adventure deserted him, and every bush, every branch of a tree took on the shape of a Cossack.

Was he, an inoffensive official, to be the first victim of the war?

He turned back and hurried towards the bridge over the Niemen.

Disillusion followed disillusion.

During the march of the army on Vilna, the rain fell in torrents and many horses perished. Their progress was difficult under a broiling sun; no more fresh meat, no more wine; the retiring enemy took the cattle with, them and emptied the cellars; nothing to drink but brackish, stinking water, and nothing to eat but a little biscuit.

Duverger is astonished at himself for having but one thought left in his head—eating and drinking; in the towns and villages all he seeks is victuals. At Dorogobouge, in a dark corner, he discovers a small bag of white haricot beans. Rejoicing over the windfall, he has some goose-fat heated and pours the haricots into it; but they harden to such a pitch that he throws them away angrily, exclaiming that he ought to have been taught the elements of the culinary art rather than a smattering of Greek and Latin. And a few weeks later, during the retreat, when he is acting as cook, and the fire he is feeding with pine-branches sends up a black and resinous smoke that gets into his eyes, and he burns a stew of horse-flesh, thereby incurring the reproaches of his comrades, he expresses the same regrets with even more anger and grief. Why, why, doesn't he know how to cook?

3

The army halts at Vitebsk and Smolensk; but the Russians perpetually evade a decisive engagement. Before Smolensk they make a stubborn defence and in order to delay the advance of the victor, they burn the suburbs. They execute their retreat steadily and in order, leaving behind them neither men nor equipages.

"We come upon houses," says Duverger, "but not a Russian; everywhere the inhabitants make off at our approach."

At last, on the 7th of September, a terrible fight takes place, and a week later Moscow displays itself before the amazed eyes of the French.

The town is entered; all is silence and tranquillity; no disorder; at the windows a few people looking timidly at the invaders.

Duverger mounts to the Kremlin and thence contemplates the conquered city. On all sides reigns a sinister silence, broken by the neighing of the horses and the march of the troops as they cross Moscow to gain their quarters.

But at night, while he sleeps, cries break forth: "Fire, fire!"

He wakes, goes down into the street; the horizon is blood-red and the fire spreading from every point, "with a sound as of distant waters in flood."

Inhabitants and soldiers run hither and thither, and by the light of the flames Duverger reads on every countenance dismay and despair.

Moreover, he feels not the slightest doubt as to the cause of the catastrophe.

He has seen men "carrying in their hands the fatal match," he has seen the men clothed in rags, "with the faces of robbers and slaves," the troops have taken in the very act and hung or shot without delay or formalities; and they were Russians.

At the end of five days, when the fire has subsided, having bivouacked a mile from the town, they go back to it, settle in, and "are busy finding quarters"; and Duverger describes the novel spectacle now presented by Moscow—pillage officially recognized; discipline disregarded; soldiers and *moujiks* removing gold, jewels and food from the ruins; dogs howling dismally and pursuing strangers who drive them off with sword-thrusts; flames bursting forth again at times in the night.

Misgiving ceased by degrees; Duverger is living in a fine palace, the only house left standing in the street; he makes the acquaintance of a young Russian who speaks German and is not afraid of the French, whom the common people looked upon as ogres and child-eaters; beneath his windows is a public promenade and a long avenue of trees; every morning he sees the Royal Italian Guards marching past to the sound of music; he goes at times to the plays at the French theatre. His meals are modest, but sufficient; he finds some figs and some macaroni, coffee and liqueurs.

One day he actually gives a dinner-party. He has discovered some wine and some white bread; from the caterer of the Guard he gets a round of beef, and, thanks to his servant, a dirty, slovenly Jew, but a good cook, he treats his guests—there were twelve of them—to soup, boiled beef, forcemeat balls fried in oil, and a larded fillet.

At dessert they drink to the coming campaign, fresh victories, and the entrance of the French into St. Petersburg!

4

On the 19th of October the army beats a retreat and Duverger contemplates with astonishment the concourse of vehicles of every description—carts, *barouches*, and *droschkis* drawn by little horses called *konias*, laboriously crossing a sandy plain. Everyone has his carriage; everyone means to carry his share of the booty back to France. One of two friends of Duverger's is taking an immense box of Peruvian bark; the other, a bookcase full of beautiful books with gilt edges and bound in red Morocco.

As for Duverger himself, he has saddled himself with jewels, furs and pictures—pictures by great masters as he believes, and which he has rolled up for convenient carrying—but he doesn't forget his own comfort; he has rice, sugar and coffee, not to mention three big pots of jam, two of cherries, and one of gooseberries.

The weather is splendid, and for fifteen days courage and confidence reign; villages are burnt, and the march goes on boldly between two hedges of flame. But mists and a fine rain foretell the approaching severity of the weather; and, on the 6th of November, the snow begins to fall.

Then begins a new kind of life—a strange, cruel, horrible life.

To be warmly dressed is essential, and Duverger wraps himself up in a woman's pelisse of yellow taffeta; the sleeves are too long for his arms, and the surplus serves him for a handkerchief.

Provisions give out, and one has to eat horse-flesh. When a horse succumbs from fatigue and hunger, it is cut up and the pieces disputed over.

Duverger pronounces horse-flesh tough, stringy, but wholesome.

But too often horse-flesh and pure water fail; then they make what they call Spartan broth.

Would you like the recipe? Here it is: Melt a great quantity of snow and so obtain a small quantity of water; sprinkle flour into it; add some fat to it, or if there is no fat to be got, some cart-grease; put in salt, or if there's no salt, powder; serve hot and eat it if you are very hungry.

Hunger appeased, Duverger and his friends lie down before a bivouac fire, sometimes on a little straw, often on the damp and frozen ground.

On waking, they find it difficult to get up; and, says Duverger, like the old horses that draw the hackney-coaches and chaises in Paris, they stagger about from foot to foot, walking unsteadily and crookedly, until the blood begins to circulate again and they get warm with walking.

It need hardly be added that many of them never rose again; that many that had risen fell by the way and, once fallen, were stripped and left naked by their comrades.

"Death," says Duverger, "took on strange manifestations. One man accosted you with a cheerful countenance and a laughing eye, pressing your hand. He was doomed. Another looked at you gloomily, uttering words of anger and despair. He, too, was doomed. But selfishness was the order of the day; friends and relations were forgotten. Hearts were broken, souls dead; they looked at one another with dull indifference, kicking away the corpse that usurped a place near the fire; angrily pushing away the dying man who fancied he had a right to fill the vacant place."

Such was the picture before Duverger's eyes for two months. He soon lost his horse, his poor Cocotte which had carried him from Mecklenburg to Moscow, and could not get used to the daily want of hay and oats.

But either on one of the treasury-wagons, or more often on foot, on he went across two hundred leagues of country, guided by nothing but the instinct of safety; ignorant of what lay to right or left of him; knowing only one thing—that the enemy was behind him; hoping only one thing—that he would reach his own country, that country which lay yonder in front of him, far, very far away.

This hope kept him up; he was fully convinced that the hour of his death had not yet struck.

He was prudent, too; he managed to keep his stores of rice and sugar and coffee for a long time, and in spite of its being forbidden by his chiefs, he sometimes lay down on the wagons, and this stolen sleep gave him fresh strength.

5

The army had once more seen Ghiatsk, Viasma and Dorogo-bouge, and was but a few days' march from Smolensk.

Duverger was sent on in advance to get horses and provisions from Smolensk and bring them back to headquarters. The approaches to the town were already crowded; Duverger had to fight with both hands and feet to get through.

In the struggle he jostles a short and rather stout man, dressed in a green pelisse and wearing a velvet cap. The man turns round. It is the Emperor.

"He addressed me very rudely," says Duverger, "and I apologized to the best of my ability, begging him to let me pass and undertaking to force a way for him. He stepped a little aside, and I went forward. At the name of the Emperor, everyone made way; that name never lost its magical influence. When overwhelmed with disasters, we cursed the Emperor; we blamed him for our sufferings; if he appeared, his prestige, the kind of halo that surrounds great men, dazzled us and every one regained confidence and obeyed his slightest wish."

After Smolensk came Krasnoï. There, as Duverger relates, took place a lengthy and bloody fight. But when the fight was over, all useless objects had to be left behind—private carriages, wagons not absolutely needed for the transport of treasure; and, to use Duverger's expression, there was a general unloading.

One left his case of Peruvian bark, the other tried to sell the library he had acquired retail, without finding a buyer. Duverger threw away his pictures nobody wanted, and made presents of his furs, wanted by everybody. During this part of the retreat, between Krasnoï and Orcha, his life was more than once in danger. He was with Claparéde's division, which had charge of the Treasury.

One day, while the convoy was passing through a ravine, the Cossacks who held the heights and had with them small guns mounted on sledges, broke the wheel of a wagon in the rearguard with a cannon-ball.

The wagon upsets and bars the pass; the paymaster-general orders Duverger to run on to warn Claparéde. The young man rushes off, in spite of his blistered feet; for his boots are so worn-out that his heels are almost on the ground; but he hastens onwards and is close to the head of the convoy, when some other Cossacks emerge from a wood and stop his way.

The soldiers who should have faced the enemy flee with cries of fright, and Duverger has only just time to throw himself into a ditch and crawl under the snow.

Presently the outcries cease, and there is silence; Duverger ventures to look around. No more Cossacks in sight; a few bold fellows have rallied and withstood them. Duverger goes on his way, finds Claparéde and tells him what has happened.

"You're a set of cowards," says Claparéde, with his usual brutality; "you tremble at a shadow of danger."

"General," answers Duverger; "if the treasury is carried off, you will have to answer for it to the Emperor."

Claparéde turns back and extricates the convoy.

The Cossacks were thus perpetually disquieting and harassing the army; they were supposed near when they were actually far away, and at the slightest sound there was a cry of "Cossacks!"

The famished Poles at times took advantage of these fears. They would come up shouting the terrible "hourra" of the Cossacks; the crowd would rush off, and the Poles, seating themselves by the Frenchmen's fires, would devour their meagre provisions.

One night, however, the Cossacks proved agreeable. Duverger was looking for a shelter in the fields, pretty far from the high road; several soldiers of the Guard were with him. They came upon a group of buildings. A Cossack sentry signed to them to go on, pointing out a barn at some distance. Not one of the Frenchmen thought of attacking the Cossack. In silence they walked on, entered the barn, stretched themselves out on clean straw, where they slept peacefully, and next day at dawn, when they set forth on their way back they saw the Cossacks going off in the opposite direction, and one who spoke French called out to them in a loud voice, "*Adieu*, you fellows, till we meet at Orcha!"

6

Duverger met the Cossacks again, not at Orcha, but on the banks of the Beresina. There, not far from Borissov, he witnessed the march past of all that remained of the Grand Army.

The Imperial Guard, already much reduced, still kept its arms, and a remnant of discipline; the other corps existed but in name; they were a confused medley of men fantastically clothed, some rigged out in the sheepskin of the peasant, some in the most costly furs; wearing tattered caps; shod with bits of linen or of leather tied on with string; carrying a stick in place of a gun, and covered with vermin which, "made lively by the warmth of the bivouac fires, ravaged their bodies and were an incessant torment."

He ought to have been able to cross the Beresina bridge without obstacle or difficulty; he was with the army treasury wagons, and the pick of the armed police had been told off to protect the convoy and prevent other vehicles from passing it; but equipages of all sorts pushed on to the approach to the bridge and mingled with the treasury wagons.

An open carriage comes up and boldly takes up a position in front of Duverger's wagon; he rushes up to drive it back and tumbles into a dry well, and here he is, thirty feet underground![2]

---

2. Lejeune, in fact, relates how in the village of Stoudienka near the bridge, officers and men were constantly falling into wells.

He shouts at the top of his voice, calling for his companions' help, and to convince them that he is worth the trouble of saving, he swears that he is safe and sound. There were college friends of his present and they threw down more or less workable ropes with a big stick tied at the end.

Duverger sits astride the stick and his friends hoist him up; he rises with outstretched arms to seize the rim of the well, but the rope breaks and he falls back again, luckily without hurting himself.

Again he shouts to his companions, entreating them not to forsake him; he recommends himself to Heaven; he registers a vow that if he escapes he will marry a girl his parents have chosen for him and who does not please him—and whom he found married on his return!

At last, with the help of fresh ropes, he is again hoisted up, and this time he gets out of the cursed well without accident.

They put him into the wagon, and, still shaken and feverish from his fall, he goes to sleep.

When he awakes, he sees the burnt bridges, and in the distance a frightful confusion; he hears the sound of artillery. During his sleep he has crossed the Beresina.

But crossing the river was not all that had to be done; there was a vast swamp to traverse in which the soil had to be strengthened with boughs of trees every dozen steps.

A league from the Beresina came a long and narrow causeway ending in three big pine-wood bridges standing one after the other above streams and bogs.

The Russians ought to have burnt these bridges, and then the French would assuredly have run the risk of danger much worse than the first.

They had left them as they were, and several years later, when Duverger wrote his *Memoirs*, he was still wondering whether the Russian generals were fools or traitors, inept or corrupt.

7

As for Duverger himself, Providence, as he says, was kind to him.

Soon after the passage of the Beresina, he meets a courier starting for France in a sledge drawn by two little horses; he makes arrangements with him and is about to take his seat beside him when a friend of the courier's gets first choice.

Next day Duverger catches sight of an overturned sledge on the road; nearby lie two dead men—the courier and his companion, murdered by Cossacks.

On trying to go to sleep one night in a barn he felt an acute pain in his eyes; his eyelids were inflamed and his sight greatly impaired; he suffered greatly the whole night through and thought he was going blind.

Next morning, as they were setting off, several of his comrades, thinking him past hope of recovery, were inclined to leave him behind; but one of them took him by the arm and laid him down on the fodder in a wagon, and, after some hours' sleep, the inflammation in his eyelids had disappeared and he had recovered his sight.

They were nearing Vilna, where there were immense stores of provisions, and the army was again to take up its quarters.

At midnight of December 9, Duverger, in his wagon drawn by seven horses, is but two leagues from the town; in another three hours he will get a good meal and a warm room.

But he comes upon another paymaster, also in charge of a wagon, and this wagon, No. 48, which contains two millions in gold, has sunk over its wheels into the snow. The paymaster begs Duverger to stay with him, and the paymaster-general, coming up, implores Duverger not to leave his colleague till the morrow.

That night, as was known later, there were twenty-eight degrees of cold.

The two men lighted a fire in a house open to all the winds of heaven and standing, for all support, on four posts.

They hadn't a morsel to eat.

The paymaster-general's cook rides past, a large sack before him.

"What have you got there?"

"Some provisions."

With one accord Duverger and his comrade knock the bag off.

The cook protests, but fearing blows, and perhaps worse—for what mattered a man more or less then?— makes off.

The two paymasters go back to their bivouac.

There they find an old sapper, whose face is pale and thin, with dull and haggard eyes, and beard hung with icicles; on his head a fur cap worn bare on one side with rubbing against the ground, his usual pillow.

"Here's something to eat," says Duverger, opening the sack, which contains rice, and flour, and fat, and a saucepan.

He discovers some wood and feeds the fire; he finds water at a spring near at hand; he cooks the rice and prepares to taste it. Hard luck! The rice is mixed with sand; Duverger has dipped the saucepan too deep into the spring and the sand has got into it. He repairs his error; using the end of his pelisse as a strainer, he obtains pure and clear water, and soon a good flour-thickened soup succeeds the sand-soup.

Then he and the other paymaster lie down upon the cook's sack, wrap themselves up in a woollen quilt and, their feet against the dwindling fire, go to sleep.

When they wake, the sapper is dead; the men they have with them to guard the wagons are dead, too; out of thirteen horses only six are still alive.

In the morning arrive men sent by the paymaster-general, who drag the wagon that holds the two millions out of the snow; it was probably the only one that managed to reach Dantzig.

Duverger's wagon stayed where it was; French and Russians pillaged it in turn.

A paymaster had accompanied the relief party of men and horses; he gave Duverger some white bread and some raw sausages.

"Fancy revelling in white bread and raw sausages!" exclaimed

Duverger.

He spent the night of December 10 at Vilna in the house of an old Jewess to whom he gave twelve eggs to make an omelette and who stole six of them. On the 11th he started for Kovno. He walked stoutly over the frozen ground, stumbling at every step, but he had the good sense not to stay in Kovno; he lost no time in crossing the bridge, and, worn-out as he was, he walked two leagues on the road to Tilsit.

Next day Marshal Ney's cook caught him up. This man had with him an enormous saucepan; for several days he lived with Duverger and his friends and won their commendation; the clever artist could serve up a dinner in less than fifteen minutes and make something out of nothing.

Before reaching Insterburg, on Prussian territory, Duverger halted at the house of a peasant.

An Italian in a discoloured and ragged uniform followed him in. He belonged to the, Neapolitan contingent that one night's cold had almost entirely destroyed. Though but nineteen years old his face was lined and fleshless. In a low voice he said something his host did not understand, which Duverger translated.

The poor wretch, his strength gone, felt his last hour was approaching and not wishing to expire in the open road, was asking permission to die under a roof.

It was at Insterburg that, for the first time for six weeks, Duverger knew the delight of eating at a table and off plates, and of sleeping in a bed.

He hastened back to France, and when once more he saw the paternal hearthstone, he was fully determined, he writes, to be satisfied with this bid for fame and to send in his resignation as an amateur warrior.

Oriot the Cuirassier

1

Charles Oriot, born in Haute-Marne and nephew of General Beurnonville, sub-lieutenant in the 10th Hussars in 1803, captain in the 9th regiment of Cuirassiers since the 12th of March, 1812, took part in the Russian expedition, and described it in a long letter to his sister which, although unfinished, is worth the trouble of reading, analysing and criticising.[1]

The beginning of the campaign was delightful. The regiment made two long halts in Prussia, one at Preussisch-Holland, the other at Eylau.

At the first, like Napoleon and Murat at Finckenstein five years earlier, Oriot went shooting the swans which swarmed on the ponds. At Eylau in the first days of June he was living in a pretty *château* half a mile from the village, and he never tired of descanting on his happiness there: enchanting country, a splendid garden; lilacs whose scent was exquisite, and as he calls it, sentimental, shaded the kiosk, the "hut" where they lived; and the band of the regiment which came two or three days a week to play its finest tunes, and, as he says again, to intoxicate him with sweet sounds.

But after Prussia came Russia, and until Moscow was reached, a daily march that seemed unending.

Oriot fought but twice—at the Moskova and in the engage-

---

1. In our *Lettres de 1812,* p. 52, we have proved that the author of the anonymous letter published by M. J. A. Leherc in 1885 (*Lettre d'un capitaine de cuirassiers sur le campagne de Russie*) was Captain Oriot,

ment at Ostrovno, which he emphatically describes as one of the greatest and most memorable of battles; still at Ostrovno he did not charge; he "stood still in the midst of the firing of the cannon."

It was the same at the Moskova. There, too, his regiment did not charge, but stood still under the rain of balls, shells and grape-shot, and sustained heavy losses. Oriot surveyed the countenances of his men, and was satisfied with their look and bearing; on the field itself, after the fashion of Napoleon, he said to them: "I am pleased with you."

Nevertheless he witnessed, as he himself says, terrible things.

Sub-lieutenant Grammont, when he was complimenting him on his coolness, answers: "I've nothing to complain of, and I only want a glass of water to drink"; and, as he speaks, a cannon-ball cuts the sub-lieutenant in two.

Oriot turns to another officer, saying how much he regrets poor Grammont; a cannon-ball kills his horse. He gets another mount, and while a cuirassier is holding his fresh horse, a shell hits the man and strikes him dead.

Oriot, covered with the earth scattered by the shell, has not even a scratch.

Whence came his coolness?

He allows that he would have preferred to charge and fight; the heat of the fray, the excitement that fills the mind, leaves no room for reflection, it is like a game of base-ball.

But to stand motionless under fire; to wait unmoved for death; to see one's comrades fall all around, wounded or dying, truly that is a thing often too much for human strength.

How then did Oriot manage to rise so courageously above all fear, all anxiety, and what his secret means for preventing tremor or shudder in the midst of battle?

He tells himself that this battle is but a lottery; that he can die but once, and it is better to die with honour than live dishonoured.

The recipe looks simple; it is not so easy to most of us as it was to Oriot.

The day after the Moskova, the French army set out for Moscow, and nothing remarkable happened till the 14th of September. The enemy abandoned its positions without making the slightest resistance. Oriot found leisure to admire the roads. What a triumph of skill they were![2] Ten carriages could drive abreast along this kind of avenue, and on each side were two rows of very tall trees with a footway for passengers between them.

The trees, resembling weeping-willows, afforded a cool shade during the great heat of summer, and in winter served as landmarks amid the snows.

During this march, Oriot felt a presentiment of coming disaster. On the 12th of September an officer of the Russian Guards came to parley; for two hours he talked with Oriot and predicted the catastrophe.

"We know as well as you do that we shall be beaten," he said; "but the winter will make us ample amends and will prove our salvation. Your courage will fail before cold and hunger. Believe me, I know the climate of my country; I hope you may not experience its malignant power."

3

At noon on the 14th of September, our cuirassier caught his first sight of Moscow, and at that sight some indefinable feeling seized him.

The city looked so strange, so marvellous, so oriental, and it was so far from France, from La Champagne!

He entered it—as he always remembered—at a quarter to three—and it took him five hours to walk through it; it seemed to him endless, and he calls it the capital of the world.

Still at moments his mind misgave him. He had seen the Emperor on foot waiting for the keys of the town and no one had

2. Oriot's words seem exaggerated; but Chambray, speaking of the Russian high roads, very wide and lined on each side with a double row of birch trees, says that this "produced a very fine effect"; and Peyrusse declares that the road leading from Orcha to Tolotchin is incontestably one of the finest in Europe, and that, laid out in a straight line, it has on each side a magnificent double row of birch trees. Cf. Castellane, *Journal*, 1, p. 192: "Those beautiful avenues of birch-trees on the high-road."

appeared to hand them over. Moreover, Moscow looked empty and deserted; in the streets and at the windows no one was to be seen but men of the people such as the army was presently to shoot or hang as chauffeurs.

Oriot's regiment bivouacked a mile away; but the next day the captain spent part of the day in Moscow. He came upon a house where some ladies who spoke French very well, gave him a most agreeable welcome; they dreaded pillage and rejoiced at having an officer in the house and willingly acquainted their guest with Russian customs.

Moscow, said Napoleon, is an extremely fine town. Oriot thought the same, and he writes that Moscow is much larger than Paris and contains innumerable mansions—five hundred more than Paris—the largest shops in the world, and a castle, the Kremlin, which alone includes at least five hundred houses.

But Oriot was strangely deceived in believing that he had come to the end of his troubles. The fire burst forth, at first in separate quarters, and then everywhere. The important shops that, according to Oriot, could have fed the invaders for two years, fell a prey to the fire; Oriot saw the people mingle with the soldiers in plundering them. He had to quit the town by streets in flames and his cloak long retained the smell of smoke.

4

The *coq rouge* was crowing in other places than Moscow. While his troop bivouacked Oriot lodged in the neighbouring village.

One night, as he lay asleep on a truss of straw, fire burst out, and the house, built like all the Russian peasants' houses, of pinewood, was speedily in flames.

Luckily a bad attack of diarrhoea had awaked Oriot; he got up and, well-nigh suffocated by the smoke, dragged himself to the door, which was opened for him by his servants.

That very day he had to set out with his regiment for Kalouga—Caligula, as Napoleon, who at times liked to be facetious, called it.

There was a river to cross. Oriot—that cursed diarrhoea!—
had gone apart for a moment. He hastens to rejoin his regiment,
falls into a hole and it is a quarter of an hour before he succeeds
in getting out of it. Moreover he is frozen with cold. No fire,
no house, and a strong wind! He undresses himself and, for two
hours, while his clothes dry, he runs up and down like a mad-
man to warm himself.

In one day he had escaped being burnt and drowned. But he
was enormously strong; his fellow-officers agreed in saying that
they knew no one whose constitution was so robust as Oriot's.

5

He spent several weeks in the famous camp at Vinkovo, called
the famine camp, which might be called also the camp of cold,
that camp where the French cavalry, already worn-out and exhausted, finally withered away.

The horses died by scores; Oriot's company had but ten
mounted men left; to get food for the beasts that were still alive
necessitated a daily journey of five or six leagues to look for a
little chaff, and for that little to risk one's life.

It was a melancholy existence, says Oriot.

But in that camp he won his cross; and if he had nothing but
horse-flesh to eat, he had, he says, one great comfort. His servant had brought him from Moscow a carriage loaded with sugar
and coffee, and day and night Oriot drank coffee and he declares
that the coffee saved his life.

Mme Fusil—the French actress who followed our troops in
the retreat, and who published the story of her adventures—was
of the same opinion; a cup of coffee was enough to warm and
revive her.

"I owe a great debt to coffee," she writes; "it was the only
thing that restored my strength; it would be possible to live a
long time on coffee alone."

Flags of truce came and went; the French hoped peace would
be made, and, as Oriot confesses, spent some pleasant hours under this agreeable delusion.

Then suddenly, on the morning of the 18th of October, a swarm of Cossacks fell upon the French camp.

"Look!" cried one of the lieutenants to Oriot; "they're close upon us!"

Oriot mounted his horse, the Cuirassiers formed into battle-line and the artillery fired grape-shot at the assailants; but the Cossacks were too many for them; they were all about, says Oriot; nothing was to be seen but Cossacks; the earth groaned under them—in front, in the rear, on the flanks, and the firing had to be on every side. So they retired, and, as Oriot adds, in good order.

It was then he performed a brilliant but useless act of prowess which earned him a wound.

With some fellow-officers he was marching behind his regiment—which now consisted of but one company, when, at a little distance, he caught sight of four Cossacks plundering a carriage.

What are four Cossacks to one Frenchman? He runs up to them and puts them to flight. Their officer appears on the scene; Oriot challenges him and pursues him into the midst of the Cossacks; he slashes the face of the first Cossack he meets, then that of the second; he pursues a third whose sheepskin he tries in vain to pierce.

But he is surrounded, hemmed in; a blow on the head from the lance of a Cossack knocks off his helmet; he catches it by the plume, and, while he stoops, the lance of another Cossack pierces his thigh. Luckily help is at hand; his comrades come up and drive the Cossacks back a quarter of a league.

"You'll always be a hussar, it seems," says the colonel when he sees Oriot again; "does a man fight like that just for fun?"[3]

Oriot's wound was a deep one; he tore up the front of his shirt as a bandage and went on riding. Ten days later he was well again.

---

3. Oriot had enlisted in the 10th Hussars in 1796 and had risen to the rank of corporal in 1798, sergeant-major and sub-lieutenant in 1803, and had not joined the 9th regiment of Cuirassiers till 1809.

6

The retreat of the Grand Army began at once, and on the 23rd of October Oriot heard in the distance the blowing up of the Kremlin; the concussion was awful, he says; it was like an earthquake.

Then came bad weather, cross-roads, many swamps, and constant attacks by Cossacks, those Cossacks the Comte de Lobau had likened to troublesome insects. Twenty thousand vehicles were burnt and the Comte de Lobau exchanged his for Oriot's. It was a splendid carriage that had cost at least a hundred *louis*; Lobau thought it too heavy, but Oriot, possessing some strong horses, finds it quite to his taste. He loaded it with sugar and coffee, cashmere shawls and lengths of cloth.

Unluckily, going downhill, a gun, driven at a gallop, caught and broke a wheel of this beautiful big carriage. Oriot had to leave it with all its contents; a little later he did not regret it, for willy-nilly he must have left it on the road.

He gives an exact description of the sort of life they led during the retreat. They marched as they pleased, and all day long by the light of burning villages, keeping up their strength by a morsel of horse-flesh. At night they lay down on the snow in some spot sheltered from the wind, and as near as possible to the bivouac-fire. Next morning, very early, they started again.

As far as Smolensk Oriot succeeded in keeping his horses, which he looked upon as the best and finest in the whole army. He had seven of them, and had refused an offer of eleven hundred francs for even one of the least good of them.

At Vinkovo or Taroutina, on the 18th of October, before rushing into the thick of the fight, he had ordered his servant to get them away from the enemy and off to the rear with all speed. So when he arrived at Smolensk he looked out for a shelter for his horses and found it in the last house but one of the outskirts—the house of a colonel of Polish hussars, where there was a stable and plenty of provender. Oriot established himself there and remained two days.

The cook was a very beautiful woman, but she made not the slightest impression on him; his heart was turned to ice, he says, and, like Castellane and many others, just then he would have preferred a bottle of poor Burgundy to the prettiest girl in the world.

He did not leave Smolensk till the Russians made their appearance; and many of our sick and wounded officers were still left in the town.

"It was necessary," writes Oriot; "it was the fortune of war; but oh! I pity those thousands of victims!"

The letter, the *grandis epistola* of the captain, ends here. But we know he was one of those who survived the miseries and horrors of the retreat.

At the Passage of the Beresina he lost the horses he had loved so dearly except the one he rode, and that was stolen from him a few days later at Vilna.

In one day he lost everything he possessed; a packed trunk, a portmanteau; a sum of two hundred and fifty *louis*; jewels of great value, and twenty-two pounds of silver he had picked up on the road.

What did it matter? He was escaping from the cold and the Russians.

"Lucky is the man," he exclaimed, "who, having been in that cursed country, succeeded in saving his skin!"

7

Before long he was re-mounted and equipped; with the pay due to him he bought three horses from his major, who was setting off for France.

The little depôt of the regiment at Elbing furnished him with a portmanteau, and to his infinite delight, he was able, for the first time for seven weeks, to change his shirt. At a small cost he bought all he needed when the effects of the dead or imprisoned officers were sold.

In the month of February, 1813, he was at Hildesheim—it was from there he wrote his letter to his sister—and feeling no ill effects from the hardships of the campaign. In fact he was twice as well as he had been before it, and he declares he feels stronger than he was when he was twenty.

He spent all his leisure in sport; friends of his in the neighbourhood gave or lent him guns and all kinds of dogs. After such a terrible ordeal wasn't a great deal of exercise the thing? He says that neither by night nor day can he keep in any hot or shut-up place, that he can't bear a fire in his room and almost always leaves his windows open.

What became of him?

He never rose above the rank of captain, although he had been through the German campaign in 1813 and the French in 1814, and, in spite of the interest of his Uncle Beurnonville, he retired from the service on the 1st of September, 1815, with a pension of 1,200 *francs* and without having reached the rank of major to which he had aspired.

Lieutenant Jacquemont

1

Porphyre Jacquemont, brother of the celebrated traveller, was a lieutenant of artillery in 1812 and went through the Russian Campaign.

At first sight the notes he kept of the journey seem of very little interest; he was not at Moscow—whatever his brother Victor may say [1]—nor at the Passage of the Beresina, and he remained in the rear of the Grand Army.

Moreover he was as calm and phlegmatic as were his father and brother, and he recounts events simply and shortly; he is writing for himself, not for other people, and intending only to put down what he wants to remember, so as to be able later to re-read the notes he has hastily jotted down on paper.

Still, a *résumé* of this note-book, short and dry as it is, will not be useless; and if, as Porphyre Jacquemont says, there is often nothing striking to record, certain details seem to us worth knowing.[2]

2

Jacquemont, attached to the Arsenal at Vilna, has spent the first part of the campaign in that town, killing time as best he can.

Sometimes he goes to the balls given by the Governor, Ho-

1. *Correspondance*, 1, pp. 40 and 192,

2. *Carnet de Route d'un officier d'artillerie*, 1812-1813, published by Victor Jacquemont du Donjon in No. 8 of the 25th February, 1899, of the Review *Souvenirs et Mémoires*.

gendorp, and in boots with spurs and riding-breeches, dances the *polonaise* and the *mazurka* with the ladies of Vilna, who all speak French. Sometimes at a restaurant kept by a compatriot called Bordais, or else at the Café de Milan, or at Esther's, the *cantinière* of the artillery, he sits at table with friends who are crossing Vilna to join the army or to return to France; and if at times he is satisfied with a couple of slices of bread and butter and a glass of rum, on certain other evenings he is a little "on."[3]

Occasionally he leaves Vilna to escort convoys of vehicles drawn by oxen or little Polish horses called *konias*.

In October he travels to Minsk, and in that wretched town can find nothing but dirty, dark streets and a number of convents and churches, staying the night sometimes with Jews, sometimes with barons. The French, as we know, called everyone who possessed a castle or a fine house a baron [4]; but Jacquemont declares that on the 3rd of November, three leagues from Smorgoni, he had lodged with a very poor peasant who actually, and with a noble air, bore the title of Baron.

As for the Jews, Jacquemont thought them disgusting, and accuses them of keeping dirty inns, working at all trades, especially usury.

3

What does he know about the Grand Army?

Very little, and like the rest of the world, he is ignorant of what is taking place further on, near Moscow, a hundred leagues away.

Eye-witnesses have told him that the battle of the Moskova was a very bloody one; that over fifty officers of the artillery

---

3. In his note-book he mentions Vieillard, who was tutor to Napoleon III and Senator under the Empire; Lebrun, who became colonel and Director of the *Musée d'Artillerie*; Morlot, who was a ship-owner at Havre and, in 1848, deputy of Seine-*Inférieure* (it was in Morlot's house at Villeneuve Saint-Georges that Porphyre Jacquemont died in 1854); the Chevalier Noizet de Saint-Paul, Jacquemont's *cousin-german*, who retired as colonel of artillery; and Emon, who defended Belfort in 1814.

4. Cf. our *Etudés d'Histoire*, 4, p. 249. Perhaps our soldiers simply Frenchified the word "*barine*"

were killed and the Cuirassiers badly mauled; that the Russians fought desperately and had lost more men than we. He hears that three-quarters of Moscow have been burnt, but that nevertheless plenty of munitions and provisions had been discovered. But it is not till much later that he hears of the retreat of the army in a letter one of his comrades receives from Fominskoe on the 9th of November.

"The nobility, the magistrates, the rich tradesmen have fled," it says; "and released prisoners, the mob and prostitutes wander about Moscow, now delivered over to them. In spite of the exertions of our men, the convicts have set fire to several quarters of the town by order of the Governor, Count Rostoptchine. Then the Emperor decided on a retreat, which began on the 16th of October with the cavalry of the Italian Guards. The army is gorged with treasures."[5]

The Grand Army is in retreat! But, like everyone else, Jacquemont does not know for certain what this retreat means. He must doubtless have had gloomy presentiments; for he notes in his diary that communication with the army is interrupted; that Vilna is snowed up; that the horses of the gun-carriages have to be roughshod; that the thermometer marks thirty degrees of frost; and on the 3rd of December he writes that a messenger has spread about "extremely unpleasant" rumours of the troops being in the greatest disorder, and having left on the banks of the Beresina more than 20,000 men and two hundred pieces of ordnance.

On the same day comes another piece of news, almost as grave.

Loison's division, which has just arrived at Vilna, is to start next day to join the army; and it is rumoured in the town that Napoleon intends to go and that Loison's division is ordered to put to flight the Cossacks who "are marching in advance of the retreating army" and wish to "seize the Emperor."

---

5. This remark recalls what Stendhal says in a letter of November 10, 1812: "The soldiers are bursting with gold *napoleons*, diamonds and pearls," See our *Episodes et Portraits*, 3, p. 260.

Isn't it strange that in Vilna, on the 3rd of December, it is guessed, known, that Napoleon proposes to leave for France?

Loison's division leaves Vilna with two detachments of artillery under the command of a friend of Jacquemont's called Lebrun. It is the 4th of December, and Jacquemont celebrates the festival of *Sainte-Barbe* by drinking a glass of punch with his friends at Esther, the *cantinière's*.

The artillery of the Grand Army in full retreat, in spite of the misery, the horrors all around them, does the same. At Bienitsa, Drouot, Pion des Loches and other officers of the Guard empty some bottles of wine, too, on the 4th of December.

But on the second day, early in the morning, Jacquemont sees Lebrun, white and haggard, come into his room.

The poor fellow had followed Loison's division, getting as far as Ochmiana, and there, on the 5th of December, at nightfall, in the market-place of the village, he had been mauled by Cossacks.

He was looking for lodgings when suddenly behind him he heard their hourra, and, thinking it a joke of the Neapolitan troopers, he turned round to answer them.

They were Cossacks—Seslavin's Cossacks—coming up at a trot. One of them made a thrust at him with his lance which he parried with his left arm but which knocked him down and pierced his hand; the rest rode over his body, and the last, to make sure he was dead, dealt him another blow with his lance, cleverly relieving him of his cape with the point of the weapon.

A little later a French officer in a sledge passed; he picked up Lebrun, whose knee was crushed.

Such was the story Lebrun told to Jacquemont at eight o'clock in the morning of December 6.

"Lay in your stores," he said; "the army will arrive tomorrow and leave nothing behind it."

The next day Jacquemont writes in his diary:

On Monday, December 7, the Emperor entered the town incognito, at about eleven o'clock. He merely changed horses and went on his way towards Kovno, without an escort, leaving behind him that which had brought him from Ochmiana. It was made up of the remnants of three regiments of Neapolitan cavalry whose endurance had given out under a night-encampment with twenty-two degrees of cold.

4

On the very day when the Emperor passed through Vilna, a small number of the survivors of the Grand Army appeared, as Lebrun had told Jacquemont would happen; then, on the 8th and 9th of December, the fugitives, clearing with difficulty the thronged gates, burst into Vilna.

But, says Jacquemont, they found all the shops closed and could not procure a morsel of bread, though the military stores were stuffed with grain and flour. Jacquemont takes the artillery officers he meets, with him, and if he can't feed them he at least gives them shelter; "they were in bad case, but anyhow they were warm."

On December 10 came orders to the troops to evacuate Vilna and to Jacquemont to blow up the arsenal. At half-past eight in the morning the fuses were placed and lighted, when, suddenly, the gunners ran away as fast as their legs could carry them.

Jacquemont pursues them, calls out to them to come back, that there is no danger—the fuses ought to last for five minutes.

But the gunners were flying from Cossacks, and the Cossacks were in time to extinguish the fuses.

So the arsenal at Vilna was not blown up and Porphyre Jacquemont missed the opportunity of connecting his name with an event that doubtless would have been one of the memorable episodes of the campaign.

A few minutes later, Jacquemont reaches the foot of the hill of Ponari. What a sight meets his eyes!

The vehicles which could not climb the hard-frozen slope are being burnt and pillaged, and so is the army-treasury; soldiers pass laden with money, and the colours taken from the Russians, the cross of St. Ivan carried off from the Kremlin [6]—the trophies, as they were called—lie scattered on the ground.

Jacquemont with his gunners climbs to the top of Ponari, and, that evening on bivouac, he sups on a smoked fish and some biscuit washed down with a drop of rum.

On December 11, in twenty-nine degrees of frost, he sets out at four o'clock in the morning, sometimes stopping in front of the houses set on fire by the fugitives to warm himself, and at ten o'clock at night, in the village of Chichmori, he lies down on the snow near a bivouac fire.

On the 12th he is at Kovno, where he drinks *schnaps* with officers of his arm of the service and sleeps in the corner of a room.

On the 13th he sleeps in a barn after eating some potatoes his men have discovered.

He passes the night of the 14th in a stable not far from Staropol and gets an unhoped-for meal; the artillery men have found a fowl and two little pigs. The golden age is come again! says Jacquemont.

On the 15th he realizes, to his great dismay that his toes are beginning to freeze a little.

On the 16th walking is very painful, but in the evening he reaches Prussian territory, and "begins to live again."

He hires a sledge, and, on the 20th, he is at Königsberg, happy at having left Russia and at last escaped from that land of misery; exclaiming that he is saved and declaring that never was there so magnificent a town as Königsberg. But Königsberg, where he stayed twelve days, was not the term of his sufferings; and the surgeon who dressed his feet did not cure him.

On January 3, 1813, Jacquemont left, to find only deplorable roads and miserable lodgings; in a village near Elbing straw swarming with lice that caused intolerable itching till he reached

---

6. Not the enormous cross that the sappers, ordered to carry it off, let fall and which broke into a thousand pieces, but a little gold cross, about six inches high, which was let into the middle of the big one. According to Castellane it had already disappeared at Krasnoï on the 15th of November.

Berlin; in an inn at the gates of Elbing, a room so crowded with soldiers that he had to sleep in the stable. Our allies, the Prussians, were already showing hostility. At Königsberg the authorities receive Murat with barely concealed coldness; in a wood near Stargard a detachment of cavalry attempt an attack on a company of French artillery; and people are daring to say that they don't want to harbour Frenchmen! It is not surprising that at Cüstrin Jacquemont caught a violent fever.[7]

He recovered by swallowing emetics, but he had a relapse at Brandeburg and was delirious. "I had a fine lot of delusions," he says; and it was the victims of such delusions that, under the maddening cold, lost their reason.

Fortunately he goes on to Magdeburg, and into the hospital there, and five days later his fever is gone.

Here ends the note-book of Porphyre Jacquemont.

The war is to begin again; the artillery is reorganized.

"My company," writes our lieutenant with his usual calmness, "was made up again; there were many missing."

5

It is a pity we have not got the letters Porphyre Jacquemont sent in 1812 from Minsk, Vilna and other places to his father, Wenceslas and his brother Victor. "I remember the letters you wrote me then," writes Victor in 1829, "as well as if they had been read to me yesterday. My ideas of war and military life were formed entirely on your experiences. On my bad days I shall think of those you spent of old, frozen and famished, and I shall never deem myself unlucky."

Wanting Porphyre Jacquemont's letters, let us accept his travel-journal; reading it carefully we shall discover more than one curious, touching and striking detail.

---

7. At Vilna, at the end of November, a malignant fever was already raging which "carried off many gunners," and the fever had taken hold of Jacquemont thirty-six hours before leaving Königsberg.

Captain Rigau

1

Captain Rigau, who became colonel of cavalry and left memoirs,[1] was in 1812 an officer on Berthier's staff.

These memoirs are little known, and perhaps it may not be useless to give here a summary of what there is in them of interest concerning the Russian Campaign. Though not abundant, the harvest is not unimportant.

Rigau was one of those Frenchmen, so numerous in those days, who thought themselves invincible; he retained an unshakable conviction that the defeat of the Grand Army was brought about by the elements and by them alone. He blindly worshipped Napoleon and abominated Rostoptchine and Hudson Lowe.

2

First of all he carries despatches to King Jerome, who is in command of the right wing of the army, and he is present at a brilliant cavalry fight, the fight at Mia, when he praises the courage of the Poles. We note that he is favourable to Jerome; he declares that the manoeuvres of the King of Westphalia were swift, that the Emperor was mistaken when he deprived his brother of the command, and that, as it was impossible for Jerome to take

---

1. *Souvenirs des guerres de l'Empire, réflexions, pensées, maximes, anecdotes, lettres diverses, testament philosophique*, the Cavalry-Colonel Rigau, Paris, 1846. The author was the son of the Brigadier-General Antoine Rigau, who was sentenced, to death by default in 1816, for having favoured the return of the Bourbons.

orders from Marshal Davout, he was right to leave the army and return to his dominions.

On his way, he takes stock of certain men of arms: General Sebastiani, "given to allowing himself to be taken by surprise," and that the men had in fact nicknamed "General Surprise"; Colonel Marbeuf, "that promising officer"; the Comte de Narbonne, whose distinction and kindness Rigau extols.

Narbonne, he writes, was one day waiting for his servant, Jean, to bring him his horse. Jean was very long in coming. At last he appeared, and as soon as he caught sight of the Count he began to bewail himself: "*Mon Dieu, mon Dieu*," said he, "what a fool I must be to keep such a good master waiting!"

All Narbonne said in his usual kindly way as he put his foot into the stirrup, was: "Don't repeat yourself, Jean; I was going to say the same thing to you—you took it out of my mouth."[2]

He has been close to Berthier and Monthion. The relations of Monthion with the staff-officers, says Rigau, were always pleasant and urbane.[3]

Berthier, under a rough exterior, had ever a warm heart. Like Napoleon, he found it difficult to get used to new faces; but he followed the careers of the officers under his immediate orders and gave them his kindly interest and protection.

As often as they started on a mission he charged them not to be taken, and, if they were, to destroy their despatches. If he did not do all the good he might have done, he never did any harm, according to Rigau.

He continually bit his nails, which gave him a vacant and pre-occupied look.

His office was a difficult one; the Emperor had him called five or six times every night.[4]

When he was told, "His Majesty wants you," he put on his

---

2. "A hedge was between Narbonne and me," says Rigau; "he did not know I could see him."
3. But in 1815 Davout says "that Monthion is foolish beyond words"; Cf. Dixen, *Mem.*, p. 262, "Monthion was a conceited person."
4. One night at Warsaw, January 8, 1807, Dedem relates, the Emperor had Berthier called as many as seventeen times.

coat, buckled on his sword, and, with his hat under his arm, preceded by an usher carrying two candles, he went to the Emperor's room.

When they said: "His Majesty wants you at once," he hurried in in dressing-gown and nightcap—a comical nightcap the officers could not look at without laughing—a cap encircled by a wide ribbon with a *chou* or rosette— and as he came back, he woke up the young men lying on the ground with: "Come, *Messieurs*, we must start."

Otherwise Rigau thought Berthier a very ordinary man. "The Emperor," he writes, "encroached upon his own glory to cloak the chief of his staff with it."[5]

3

The beginnings of the campaign did not appear very brilliant to Captain Rigau. He recounts how the army marched through melancholy, gloomy forests, over shifting sands, in overwhelming heat greater than that in Italy and Spain; that in less than thirty leagues from Kovno to Vilna, they had lost nearly five thousand horses [6]; that there they suffered from incessant rains; that the Russians, setting everything on fire, left very few resources behind them; that the "very existence of the men had become a problem," but that never did any army more heroically endure fatigue and privations.

He was at the battle of the Moskova, and the day before had seen the Emperor ride in front of his troops to discover the enemy's position, and the veterans crowding to the Imperial tent

5. Compare this portrait with that drawn by Stendhal (A. Chuquet, *Stendhal-Beyle*, p. 381; and with Dedem's *Mem.* p. 262, "Berthier was beginning to age"; and with what Baltazard says on the 24th of January, 1813: "He is in a state of health which gives rise to fears for his life, and little or no hope of his being able to continue his duties."

"Berthier," says Planat, "was incapable of undertaking an important command; but as he was the habitual interpreter of the Emperor's plans and ideas, it was thought he would preserve their tradition and act in accordance with them; but after the disaster at Vilna, we saw that he was no good."

6. Others said ten thousand, and Matthew Dumas, the intendant-general, said seven thousand.

to look at the portrait of the King of Rome Bausset had brought from Paris.

As for the battle itself, which he describes as immense and gigantic, he makes no criticism; he looks upon it as "one of the Emperor's greatest feats of arms."

He admires Moscow. "This town," he says, "excites more wonder than any other in Europe; it has not the monotony of London and other capitals; the weary traveller revives at its sight; it reminds one more of the East than of the West; yet one can get some idea of it by picturing five hundred of the most beautiful and sumptuous *châteaux* surrounded by small towns, villages or country-houses, so immense are the gardens, as well as the commercial establishments. It is the mart of Asia and Europe."

Like all the narrators of the campaign, he describes the feeling of joy and pride that filled all hearts at the look of this Promised Land.

"The look of the gilded cupolas, the belfries surmounted by the Greek cross, encircled by little chains waving like wreaths in the air, electrified the imagination of the army and brought hope to the spirit, mingled, as was allowable after such toil and glory, with a touch of pride. The thoughts of many of us flew back to the past. Mine went back to Oporto."

He is given the command of one of the quarters of Moscow and takes measures to maintain order; but the fire speedily breaks out, and, for some days, the army quits the town whose destruction appears inevitable.

On the night of September 17, Rigau, returning from some mission, and ignorant of the abandonment of Moscow, seeks everywhere for the staff-officer.

"I was well-nigh suffocated by the violence of the wind, by the smoke and the rarefaction of the air caused by the heat of the fire. Moscow looked like a pit surrounded by a sea of flames; they reached from the North to the South, rising to the skies; the sound of the sheets of iron crashing down from domes and houses on to the wide pavements struck sadness into the heart. It is certain that Rostoptchine will go down to posterity as the author of this infamous deed; and indeed it would be a pity if his name were forgotten and so pre vent the eternal execration of such a monster. It is to be hoped that a suitable punishment waits him and Hudson Lowe, the bull-dog and gaoler of St. Helena."

Rigau regretted the long stay Napoleon made in Moscow. Since the city was burnt, he held, he says, "that the army ought to be given eight days to rest and eat, and then, before the setting in of the great cold, return to the Niemen. In that case our fate would have been very different; a prudent retreat, which is not the consequence of a defeat, takes nothing from the victory gained. Besides, the Russians would have cursed Rostoptchine all the more deeply, for the burning of Moscow would have been to no purpose."

Berthier ordered him to keep with Marshal Mortier, who was to stay to the last in Moscow to blow up the Kremlin.

"I stayed, therefore, with the Due de Trévise until he rejoined the Emperor at Vilna. As we left Moscow, we heard the explosion of the mine, but I doubt if it did much damage to the Kremlin."

Here is an anecdote of the march from Moscow to Vereza. Marshal Mortier was very angry with a soldier who shot at a crow.

"Why," said Rigau to the man, "did you lay yourself open to reproof, and a crow isn't good eating anyhow, is it!"

"Hunger would have made me think it good," answered the other.

Another anecdote.

Rigau, on foot in the midst of a crowd of jaded and almost unarmed men, caught sight of a very small and swarthy officer walking beside three guns and smoking the short pipe the soldiers called a *brule-gueule*. The man, who appeared to be a lieutenant of artillery, was wearing a blue great-coat with a cape that reached his elbows and a hat edged with a narrow plain ribbon.

Suddenly a group of Cossacks appears on the horizon; the

officer perceives Rigau, calls him comrade, begs him to get together as many men as possible to mask his guns, which he at once turns on the enemy, leaving room to take aim.

The Cossacks come within firing distance; the officer takes aim, fires one of his pieces, and the ball falls into the very midst of the Russians, who make off as fast as they can. The column goes on its way, and Rigau, congratulating the gunner on the accuracy of his fire, learns that he is General Allix, whose bit of a pipe is still alight.[7]

From Vereza to Smolensk the army endures "many hardships difficult to describe and too painful to recall."

It hears of Malet's "prank" and already foresees "the departure, as near as urgent, of Napoleon."

Moreover, the Emperor "showed more solicitude for his soldiers than had been his wont in any of his campaigns. He would stop when he caught sight of a sick and wounded man walking with difficulty, and not leave him until he felt sure there was a possibility of saving him by putting him on one of the gun carriages."

At Krasnoï Rigau loses his brother-in-law, Major Vilmain, formerly *aide-de-camp* to Bernadotte, "one of the best and most capable of officers."[8]

At Orcha the troops found shops and food, and rations were given out. Then came a thaw, and this thaw eased some of the troubles of the army and made it almost forget the severe cold that had crushed it since leaving Smolensk, and the bivouacs less unbearable.

But it did not last long; the cold returned; the winter grew more terrible than ever, and of the seven horses Rigau had possessed when he crossed the Niemen not one was left; at Orcha he had had to kill the last to feed his comrades; "no sooner was

---

7. See Bodenhausen's report (*Mem.* of King Jerome, 6, p. 16): "On the 15th of November, at Krasnoï, Allix, having only four pieces of ordnance left, and not enough gunners, himself served the guns with the help of the officers still left standing."

8. Vilmain, born at Spincourt in la Meuse in 1771, lieutenant and then captain in the 3rd battalion of la Meuse; *aide-de-camp* to Bernadotte in 1806, had been a major since 1807 and in 1804 had joined the 53rd regiment.

it cut up than we filled our pockets and nose-bags with bits of its flesh."

The Beresina is crossed, and Rigau gives enthusiastic praise to the sappers; they showed, he says, "an heroic devotion—quite superhuman; they all perished, sacrificing their lives; their sole motive being honour and obedience to duty."

He gives praise also to the Guard.

"The march of the Emperor, surrounded by his Guard, was, in spite of all our misfortunes, a majestic sight.

"The soldierly and sorrowful countenances of his grenadiers looked all the finer and more striking because of the grief in their hearts. A superhuman strength inspired these strongly-tempered spirits, upheld by their devotion. They halted but to fall down and die, faithful and uncomplaining; all their anxiety was for the Emperor.

"The whole world must render homage to these Guards; they understood the grandeur of their mission; they felt they were the flower of the nation and the army."

The Emperor left the army at Smorgoni on the 5th of December. But Rigau approves of his action: "The Emperor has acted on the best advice"; he alone "could hasten the formation of the fresh forces necessary to replace our losses"; he alone could "expedite new resources," and, adds Rigau, "as for myself, I was relieved of a great weight when I knew the Emperor was gone and out of danger."

After Smorgoni, came Vilna, and then Kovno. But they only passed through Vilna. "There," says Rigau, "I was greatly grieved by the death of the brave General Dornès, who succumbed to fatigue and old wounds. He was in command of a brigade of *cuirassiers*, and was a fine soldier; an honour to the army."

At the end of his story, Rigau makes the following remarks:—

Posterity will look on it as a fable that an army, exhausted with hunger, thirst, sickness, a fatal climate, a most unusual winter, even for Russia, should have endured a retreat lasting several months, in which, in the midst of forests and deserts men perished by thousands, wandering through snow and ice; while Death in his most terrible forms pursued men who were nothing but skeletons, but who yet found strength to conquer when the enemy believed them at any moment an easy prey. The elements alone vanquished us; and we had to fight the best of soldiers save ourselves; for the Russian soldier is sober, patient, tough, religious—if somewhat idolatrous and superstitious—bearing round his neck a picture of St. Nicholas, and knowing how to die uncomplainingly.

Major Pion

1

Pion, born at Pontarlier in 1770, and, as the youngest of seven children, destined for the church, entered the Seminary at Besançon in 1789, and some months later, in 1790, he was already a professor in the college of his native town and head of the establishment. One got on quickly in the days of the Revolution.

But he refused to take the oath of the Civil Constitution of the clergy, so incurring the persecution of the patriots, who imprisoned him at Lons-le-Saunier, where he had taken refuge, and afterwards put him under supervision. So in 1793 he obeyed the call to arms and joined the army.

Entered in the School of Artillery at Chalons, 1795, from that time he followed the military career, it must be owned, with no great enthusiasm.

In his *Mémoires* [1] he describes with striking sincerity his impressions of war.

Sent from Chalons to Strasbourg and thence to the Fort of Kehl, which the Austrians had invested and were bombarding, he owns his perplexity and awkwardness.

What's the good of mathematics? He doesn't know even how to turn a gun-carriage, or repair a breast-work. "A warning to *Messieurs les Élèves* who join the corps with heads stuffed with x and y!"

---

1 *Mes Campagnes* (1792-1815), *Notes and Correspondence of Colonel Pion des Loches of the artillery*, arranged and published by Maurice Chipon and Léonce Pingaud.

But he soon gained the needful coolness, confidence and experience. He was at the siege of Peschiera and in the campaigns of 1805, 1806 and 1807. In 1805 he remarks on the knavish tricks of the generals and the wastefulness of the soldiers, who destroyed everything, spilling the flour about the houses and the wine in the cellars.

In 1806 he is present at the Battle of Jena and owns that to him it was quite incomprehensible: "Where were we? What part of the battlefield did we occupy? Who was at our right or at our left? I haven't the slightest idea even now."

It was the same at Eylau. He hears the firing but sees nothing; all he knows is that the weather was mild and there was a thaw; that the horses sank up to their bellies in the snow; that the sun shone at times; that there was a violent wind; that the snow blinded the combatants, and that the next day he was not surprised to learn that Augereau's corps had gone astray amongst the Russians and had been roughly handled by them.

He returned to France by Berlin, where terrible poverty reigned; Prussian officers implored his help, and an aged captain of seventy, formerly one of Frederick's soldiers, asked him for alms.

Pion then, with the rank of captain, joins the foot artillery of the Imperial Guard. He fights in Spain and in Russia, and the chapter of his *Souvenirs* devoted to the campaign of 1812 is perhaps the most interesting in the book.

On his return in 1813 he was made Major of the 2nd regiment of Artillery at La Fère. At Villette, in 1814, he fired his last shot. In 1815, on hearing the news of Napoleon's landing, he won over the wavering d'Aboville and shut the gates of La Fère in General Lallemand's face.

He had his reward; Louis XVIII gave him the rank of colonel and ennobled him.

Thenceforth Pion styled himself the Chevalier Pion des Loches, and when he died in 1819 he left behind him the reputation of a pure and ardent champion of the throne and altar. Soldier in his own despite, Pion detested war. He has no love for his profession—"a convict's trade"—and he remains in the service because he "must complete his career." Had he not said that "at the present time an honest and sensible man is not made for the profession of arms!" And in 1803 he had applied for a post as Professor in the School of Fontainebleau and of Collector of Taxes in Franche- Comté.

He is an original figure; a soldier of Napoleon who is not dazzled by the victories and conquests that cause the hearts of succeeding generations to beat, and the great events in which he takes a part—however small a part—apparently do not move him. He pities the vanquished; he deplores the wrongs done under his eyes by the army; he sees, with regret and disgust, men with neither education nor principles promoted over his head; but he has no ambition; he despises intrigue; he will not "sue for the patronage of the great or buy their favours by cringing."

He has still, he says, a bit of religion about him, and he never loses the stamp of the Seminary.

At Metz in 1802, when they hear of the restoration of Sunday, his fellow-officers ask him jestingly to become their chaplain.

Assuredly he was one of the best-educated officers in the Imperial army; jotting down in Latin the events of his life; speaking Latin "to his heart's content" in Germany with the *curés* and *pasteurs*; respectfully visiting the ruins of the house where Catullus had lived with Lesbia; making his men in 1815 take an oath consisting of four verses from *Athalie*; fond of dissertations; devoting a long digression in one of his letters to the subject of interest on loans.

One can understand his companions looking upon him as a marvel and a queer fish.

2

The portion of his writings concerning the campaign of 1812 is vividly interesting.

Even before reaching Russia, Pion foresees the disastrous results of the expedition. There is no fodder for the horses; as usual there is no order or administration; the army must live by the sword, and even on Prussian territory and with their allies, the troops pillage atrociously, as if they were in an enemy's country.

The Niemen is crossed, and Pion is already wishing the war was ended, and that he were on the other bank of the river on his way back to France.

The nights are icy-cold, killing a third of the horses, and the troops suffer fearfully from the storm of the last days of June.

"We have gone through a bivouac such as no army has ever experienced; for forty-eight hours an appalling cold rain fell in torrents."

From the moment he reaches Vilna, he foresees that if the Emperor proceeds further it will be to his own hurt and detriment. On the way from Vilna to Vitebsk, he notices that the soldiers scatter to look for provisions.[1] At Vitebsk, Smolensk and Viasma he realizes that the intention of the Russians is unmistakably to deprive the invader of resources; to entice the French army as far as possible, and to crush it when it is perishing of cold and hunger.

His comrades in arms already see the Emperor entering Moscow and dictating terms of peace. Pion tells them they are blind, and like Hagen saying to the Niebelungen that never will they see Burgondian country again, he tells them quietly that never again will they see France; and they call him a bird of ill omen.

At the Moskova, on September 7, like Boulart,[2] on all sides he hears a terrible cannonade, and only at intervals through the smoke discerns the position of the enemy. Like Boulart, he is close to Napoleon and, from the beginning of the action till four o'clock in the afternoon, he never takes his eyes off him.

"The Emperor," he writes, "did nothing but walk about in a state of agitation, listening to the reports of the start officers and generally waving them back without uttering a single word."

When Pion arrives at Moscow he has not fired a single cannon. He enters the town, walks over a great part of it, and, seeing

---

1 This relaxation of discipline had not escaped Napoleon's notice: "They rush helter-skelter after victuals," he wrote at that time to Berthier.
2. See the following chapter.

scarcely a soul about, feels terror-stricken. In the evening he is offered hospitality in a French household, and at the house of his compatriots, met by chance, he makes the best meal of his life—vermicelli soup, rib of beef, macaroni, Bordeaux, and coffee; and the mistress of the house assures him that he will find Moscow very pleasant, that he will get quarters in a palace, and that the city is a city of luxury and riches.

Suddenly his host, who has gone out, appears, wild with terror,

"*Messieurs*, the Bourse is on fire! What is the Bourse? A building bigger than the Palais Royal."

Moscow is a prey to fire: Pion, in his *Souvenirs,* dwells strongly on the scenes of pillage. He sees the streets strewn with books, china, furniture and clothing of all sorts; he sees the army utterly demoralised, and on every side drunken men loaded with spoils; he sees the officer in charge of the gate of Moscow on the Petrovski road levying a duty on all booty brought out by the military, and heaping up baskets of eggs and bottles of wine in his guard-room.

The fire subsided. There is a return to Moscow and taking up of quarters. Pion, established in Prince Bariatinskys palace, and with the rank of major, keeps open house; his fellow-officers dine sumptuously with him and drink the most delicious wines. But he is never in agreement with his guests, who fancy that the Tsar will make peace, while he calls them simpletons and blames their credulity in trusting to wild rumours.

How can they believe that after having led the French on into the very heart of the Empire, after having deprived them of all means of resistance, Alexander would lay down his arms?

He foresees that the army must speedily retreat, and he makes preparation by buying some excellent furs and piling his baggage-wagon with provisions.

His presentiments prove correct; on the 18th of October on parade at the Kremlin, while the Emperor is reviewing the third corps, comes Bérenger, an *aide-de-camp* of the King of Naples, who whispers to his friends: "Things are going badly"; and the

Emperor, reading the despatch he has brought, learns of the re-pulse at Vinkovo and Taroutino.

Next day they set off, and two or three weeks later, the retreat has degenerated into a rout. Each man marches as he pleases and looks to his own safety; the artillery burns its ammunition and its gun-carriages; the soldiers cast away their knapsacks and their arms; many of them fall into the hands of the Cossacks foraging far away from the high-road; others die of cold and hunger.

Thanks to his baggage-wagon, neither Pion nor his friends suffer from hunger at first; but the Emperor decrees that the amount of baggage must be diminished at all costs and that half the vehicles must be burnt. So the precious baggage-wagon has to be abandoned, and so as not to lose the hundred and fifty bottles of wine and liqueurs it contains, they are drunk, and what was to have been the consolation of several days disappears in a few hours.

One major has kept his canteen; but at Smorgoni, on the 5th of December a gunner steals it, and, caught in the act, smashes the bottles against the wheel of a carriage in a rage.

Major Boulart, Captain Oriot and Mme Fusil all declared they owed their lives to coffee; Pion owed his to sugar; during the Retreat he lived entirely on sugar, eating more than a pound of it a day; his palate is raw with it. However, he kept wonderfully well, and could have said, like Napoleon, that his health had never been better—if it hadn't been for his boots!

Since leaving Smolensk, he had not dared to take off his boots for fear of not being able to get them on again. The frost had made them shrink, and for the first few steps he took in the morning he was obliged to walk on the toe or the heel or the side of the boot, so as to bend the sole. His feet swelled, and he could not sleep at night for the atrocious pain in them. At last, on the 15th of December, at Vilkoviski, he got his boots taken off by a servant of the post-house.

The sturdy Pole could not succeed at first, and proposed cutting up the accursed boots; but a five-*franc* piece gave him strength and courage; he set to work again and his efforts were crowned with success.

Pion's feet were black and numb, but the skin was not broken. How he sighed with relief and comfort as he put on a pair of furred shoes? On the same day he crossed the Russian frontier.

3

In Pion's story there are several personages who especially claim the attention of the reader: Sorbier, Drouot, and Napoleon.

Sorbier is commander-in-chief of the artillery of the Imperial Guard. He is the harsh, hard and peremptory Sorbier painted by Major Boulart; the Sorbier Lejeune describes as hot-headed; the man who at the Moskova, when he receives orders to bring up his guns, does not leave the *aide-de-camp* time to deliver his message but exclaims impatiently:

"I've been waiting for you more than an hour!"

Pion quotes some of Sorbier's speeches. At times the general's language was of an exceedingly vigorous and crude character.

Before Vilna, when the celebrated storm burst, he boldly declared that it was madness to attempt such ventures; and when Pion complained of the loss of his gun-carriages: "You're put out at the loss of your guns," says Sorbier; "I don't care a rap; it's quite immaterial whether you lose them today or tomorrow; all the better for the gunners who work themselves to death trying to save them; in spite of all the trouble you're taking, not a single one of your carriages will get to the Niemen."

At Fontainebleau, on the 1st of April, 1814, he says to General Neigre, the superintendent of artillery, who applies for cloth for cartridge-cases: "*Parbleu*, Neigre; you can do what you please about it. This is what that fellow has brought us to after twenty-five years of revolution, and there's nobody found to put a bullet into him!"

This is the Sorbier who, under the influence of Lallemand, mortifies and humiliates Drouot, accusing him of wanting both ability and zeal, of managing his guns with less intelligence than the lowest corporal in the regiment, and of always pushing himself forward.[3]

Pion is equally severe on Drouot. According to him, Drouot is an egoist, a hypocrite devoured by ambition and thinking only of his own advancement; during the Retreat he keeps his provisions to himself, and, at the Passage of the Beresina, he makes haste to get across the river without a thought of his companions or his horses.

But, like Lallemand, Pion is jealous of Drouot, who, "in one year, becomes First officer of the Legion, Count, General of Division, Adjutant and Major-General of the Guard," and who, in 1815, is "the second person of the Empire"; and, in consequence, Pion refuses to see any merit in him.

Yet he himself had twice said that Drouot bore "a high reputation" in the army, and that that reputation ought "to win him the rank of general."

Had he not said also that on the 4th of December, the feast of *Sainte-Barbe*, at Bienitsa, this Drouot he calls close-fisted, distributed bottles of wine to his fellow-officers!

As we know from other witnesses, Drouot did more than his duty during the Russian campaign, and did he not write that the loss of his poor gunners, whom he had seen die of cold and hunger, tore his heart?

When he was given the rank of general, he declared he was sorry for the promotion; he was content with his rank as a colonel and had no wish to rise above it.

And what involuntary praise Pion gives Drouot in his report of one of their conversations during the retreat.

"Misfortunes sometimes make for good," says Drouot; "after this campaign the Emperor will mix some water with his wine; he will be satisfied with the fame already won and run after no further adventures. He was beaten by the elements, not by the Russians. Well, then, he can make peace and give up the right bank of the Rhine without dishonour."

Through the Revolution, as under the Empire, Pion had al-

---

3. "Sorbier," says Planat, "was a man of medium height, thin and sallow, of harsh, forbidding aspect, and what in military slang is called a nasty customer."

ways remained a Royalist, always loved and regretted the Bourbons. When he meets Drouet, who had been called the jailer of Louis XVI, now the *sous-préfet* of Sainte-Ménehould, he shudders with indignation; there never was, according to him, a person with such a frightful countenance, and he is furious at the sight of the ribbon of the Legion on the breast of a man whom he thinks unworthy of respect.

At Dresden he is amazed that the King of Saxony—so pious, so devout a man—can be the friend of Napoleon.

When, on the 9th of April, 1814, in a café at Amboise, he finds the first newspaper bearing the shield of France and the three *fleurs-de-lis*, he feels like one born blind whose eyes have been opened. On the following 17th of May, when at the Tuileries the King and his august family walk through the rooms to go to Mass, Pion's eyes fill with tears at the cry: *Vive le Roi!* bursts from his lips.

On January 21, 1815, at La Fère, without any order from the Ministry and without communicating his intention to any one, he reads out to his men the will of Louis XVI; and if, after the return from Elba, he stays on with his regiment and does not emigrate to Ghent, it is solely in order to restrain the *canaille* of La Fère and not leave the place open to the Jacobins.

Pion, as he says, had never had any love for either person or the rule of Napoleon, and he foresaw and looked forward to his fate. From the beginning of the year 1812 he had asserted that the Russian expedition would entail the ruin of the Emperor, and in the November of 1813, when he was asked how things would end, he boldly answered: "Bonaparte will be dethroned; by Christmas his reign will be over."

In consequence his verdict on Napoleon's role in 1812 is a very severe one, sometimes rightly so, sometimes unjustly.

He calls the Emperor the greatest fool in the world; he styles him a deserter and taunts him with having left his army at the mercy of all the freaks of the adventurer Murat; he maintains that Napoleon "gloated over" the sight of his disorganized troops, and adds in this connexion that several soldiers: "Cursed Napoleon at the top of their voices."

Is it worthwhile to refute him on these points?

Need we answer, with Ségur, that if there were curses, they were never uttered in the Emperor's presence, and that, amidst so many ills, the worst still seemed to be displeasing him?

Must we repeat with Fantin, that from the ranks of the army came no single murmur, and that if the Emperor no longer heard the shouts of love and enthusiasm that welcomed him of old, censure at least was spared him?

In one passage of his *Souvenirs* Pion complains that under the Empire his promotion had been "slow and slight." May we not gather that if he had won the same measure of promotion as Drouot, he might have spoken of Napoleon in gentler terms?

Major Boulart

1

Major in the artillery of the Guard, with the rank of colonel in the line, officer of the Legion of Honour and Baron of the Empire, le Rémois Jean Francois Boulart, who was to be promoted to general of brigade in 1813, and who commanded the artillery in the Army of the Rhine in 1815, made the Russian campaign,[1] and told its story, and was during the retreat one of those dauntless men who, as Napoleon said, never seemed to be put-out or to lose their good-humour and energy.

2

He leaves Mayenne on March 16, 1812—for, for us, remarks Boulart, Mayenne meant France—and on May 29 arrives at Posen, having met with nothing of interest on the way; since to the soldiers, as he says, towns that evoke no great memories are but military land-marks, sign-posts, even simply inns.

At Thorn, on June 5, the Emperor reviews the artillery, and talks with Boulart and others in the gay, familiar and charming fashion of his when he was not pre-occupied. A captain ventures to ask for a post as Director of Indirect Taxes for his brother-in-law, who was not even an official in the Administration, and Napoleon grants the request. Boulart is bold enough to say that with such troops and such guns as that of the Guard, the Emperor could march to the conquest of India; and Napoleon smiles.

---

1 *Mémoires Militaires du Général baron Boulart*, pp. 238-283.

No one dreamed that the campaign could come to grief; full of enthusiasm and faith in the genius of their chief, all repeated after the Emperor that Russia was doomed. "We'll celebrate the 15th of August at St. Petersburg!" cried Boulart.[2]

But who would not have believed in victory when the army had crossed the Niemen, when on every side sprang up battalions and squadrons as if they had risen out of the ground? A magnificent, an unique spectacle!

A storm burst; rain fell in torrents; the thunder growled and flashes of lightning pierced the clouds without a break; battalions and squadrons kept on the move, and this vain unloosing of the powers of the heavens against the earth made, says Boulart, a most imposing spectacle.

3

Thus the French entered Russia, proud of their strength and certain of success; but their tone soon changed. Nature began to turn against them; first came unbearable heat, as great as in Madrid, Boulart reports; then on June 29 came a fresh and awful and extraordinary storm; such a terrible tempest had not been known in the memory of man.

Thunder and lightning burst forth from every side of the horizon; soldiers were struck dead; torrents of rain flooded the bivouacs; the downpour lasted all the next day. This was the first of the disasters. With incredible difficulty they had to make their way over cut-up roads, and those who had fought in 1807 had fresh experience of the thick and sticky mud of Pultusk.

Worst of all was the loss of horses; nearly ten thousand perished. On June 30, when he reached Vilna, Boulart had lost ninety draft-horses and seventy of the little ponies of the country.

He had not had time to bring a store of oats from Thorn, and the poor beasts had nothing to eat but the still-green wheat, the most unwholesome food they could have had in the state of overwork in which they were constantly kept. The green food

---

2. Boulart does not quote this speech; it is reported by Pion (*Mes Campagnes*, p. 282).

had weakened them; the glacial rain finished them off.

The artillery of the Guard renewed its teams at Vilna, and on July 31 they bivouacked in the neighbourhood of Vitebsk; but they were tired out with marches over muddy roads through woods, and they had not yet fired a shot.

Would the Russians flee onwards for ever without standing their ground? Would the battle they longed for never come off? Moreover, Boulart thought it would be wiser to go no further. He remembered that the bad weather begins early in Russia, and believed it would be more prudent not to undertake a further advance, but to take up permanent quarters at Vitebsk, and next year push on into the heart of Muscovy.

For a moment he half thought this plan would be accepted; the Emperor had some houses pulled down to enlarge a square where the daily parade took place. Who knows that he had not some idea of restoring the Kingdom of Poland? That was the ardent desire of the Lithuanians.

Boulart was living in a country house some miles outside Vitebsk, and the mistress of the house told him she detested the Russians, and if Napoleon proclaimed the independence of Poland, the Lithuanians would rise in a body and help him to their utmost; but that if he kept silent, anxiety would take hold on them and put a stop to the enthusiasm of the people.

But who takes up winter-quarters at the end of July or the beginning of August?

Napoleon hadn't come from Paris to sit down at Vitebsk, and when, on parade, he invested Friant with the command of the grenadiers of the Guard, he spoke these words: that he should always keep the grenadiers under his own eyes, and that General Friant, whom he still needed, would continue to lead his division during the campaign.

On August 13, after a ten days' rest which, as reports another member of the expedition, had done great good to both the bipeds and the quadrupeds of the army,[3] the Guard left Vitebsk, and by forced marches reached the shores of the Dnieper, the

---

3. Fantin des Odoards, *Journal*, p. 315.

ancient Borysthenis whose name revived Boulart's *Memories of the Classics.*[4] On the 17th it appeared before Smolensk.

A desperate fight took place under the walls of the fortress; but it was not the battle the French had longed for, nor was it the victory they were in haste to gain and which was to end the war.

"God grant we may at last have the good fortune of coming up with the enemy we have been pursuing so long!" exclaimed Drouot.

But they did not come up with the enemy's army; once more it stole away, and the Russians who were defending Smolensk held out till nightfall and on retreating set the town on fire.

On the top of the ramparts their figures stood out against a background of flames like dissolving views, and Boulart's spirit was filled with a profound sadness.

Evidently the enemy was exasperated and would not make peace so easily. Next day, when he went into Smolensk, his heart was torn at the sight; houses burnt down or still burning on every side, ruins and corpses everywhere, the inhabitants taking refuge in the churches and looking at the French with hostile or despairing eyes.[5]

Once more arose the question, would Napoleon halt at Smolensk?

He had appeared, Boulart declares, to have no other aim but the crossing of the Dnieper and making a left wheel fall upon the rear of the Russian army to cut it off from Moscow. He

---

4. The Borysthenis, with its sonorous name, appeared to the French a mean sort of river; some of them said of it: "Seen from afar, it's something, but from near, just nothing at all"; and Peyrusse writes: "This river has been much extolled; I don't think it comes up to its reputation." And another writes: "We reach the shores of the Dnieper, so here is the ancient Borysthenis! There's nothing remarkable about its banks, and it isn't more than three or four hundred feet wide. All one's illusions about this ancient limit of the East vanished at the sight of the beggarly reality. A glance was enough!"

5. Cf. in our 1812, *La guerre de Russie, notes et documents*, vol. 1, p. 61, a letter from an officer: "Never shall I forget the sight of the interior of Smolensk; picture to yourself all the streets, every square heaped with dead or dying Russians, and the flames all round lighting up this awful picture."

arrived too late; but the taking of Smolensk, adds Boulart, was an important advantage, and Smolensk would make excellent head-quarters; as the Comte de Lobau had said to Napoleon: "Smolensk is a fine position for cantonments."

But the Emperor pushed on towards Moscow.

In his fifteenth bulletin he writes that the taking of Smolensk, Smolensk the Sacred and the Strong, has had a very depressing effect on the minds of the Russians; that the people looked upon it as the key to Moscow and that the peasants were constantly repeating: "Whosoever owns Smolensk, owns Moscow."

But the march of the French army was again very fatiguing; the heat was intense, and as the Russians retired, they set fire to the towns and villages on their way.

"Since we left Smolensk," reports a French officer, "I have been constantly surrounded by flames."

4

At last, on September 7, at Borodina, the battles so long desired and looked forward to, took place.

The Emperor was in front of the Redoubt of Chevardino, captured two days earlier; behind him was massed the Guard, looking its finest, and Boulart, standing at a little distance, could observe him at his ease.

For a great part of the day, the Emperor stayed there, walking to and fro, his hands behind his back, or standing still and resting. Sometimes calling for Berthier; sometimes giving instructions to his officers or listening to their reports; sometimes talking with wounded generals who came up from time to time.

Around the Emperor and amongst the Guard reigned a silence which was a strange contrast to the appalling noise of the battle. Through the dust and smoke, the movements of the troops could be dimly seen, and little by little the success of our attack was learnt. But it was known, too, that the field had been bought dear and the taking of the redoubt had cost much blood.

Those around tried to discover what the Emperor was thinking; they wanted to see his face grow cheerful, light up as it used to do; such a brightening would have been the sign of an undoubted and complete victory; but he remained gloomy and anxious.

At last the Guard was ordered to advance, and there was something serious and solemn about its moving; it seemed as if on it must depend the issue.

Suddenly it came to a halt.

Once more Boulart had not fired a shot, and he owns that he was struck with amazement.

From afar he had seen the Russians effect their retreat without disorder, and he said to himself that the French army had fought in vain and, after so long drawn-out and bloody an action, gained nothing but a position.

On the 14th, from a height, he gazed at Moscow with its gilded domes and its innumerable cupolas of every colour; he wondered at the Asiatic aspect of the city; he thought how, after eight hundred leagues of journeying, after so many privations and hardships, he was looking upon the cradle of this great Russian Empire, the ancient capital of Muscovy, the Holy City; he tells himself that he has reached the end of his troubles; this is the Promised Land, the oasis after the desert.

5

That very night the fire broke out; a fire which in a short time spread beyond belief.

On the 15th Boulart entered the town, placed his guns in an immense square not far from the Kremlin, and had the neighbouring houses searched and watched, for he knew already the prisons were thrown open and he had caught sight of chauffeurs of hideous and ferocious aspect.

But the fire spread and reached the quarter where Boulart had established himself, and sparks carried by the wind fell close to his guns.

Our major received no orders, and it was the most restless night he had ever spent.

On the 16th, at dawn, he went to the Kremlin, running great

risks; at times passing under a canopy of fire; hearing the sinister sound of metal plates falling continually from the Palace roofs; sometimes struck by falling fragments; surrounded by dense smoke; closing his eyes for the intense heat of the flames as they came near him; scarcely able to see his way, urging on his trembling horse when it refused to go forward.

At last he emerges from the burning zone, crosses a quarter in absolute ruins and reaches the gates of the Kremlin. He enters, and sees nothing but countenances full of dismay; discouraged and doubting men; and General Curial orders him to follow the Emperor, who is leaving the Kremlin and Moscow.

Boulart followed the Emperor and the Guard to the castle of Petrowski. Two days later he returned to the town and, with the Guard, took up his quarters near the Kremlin.

He wanted for nothing; he had a good cook, Jarlot from Laon, and he feasted his friends richly.

But there was no stopping in Moscow; on October 19 they set forth again, and Boulart was glad to go southward, towards a new country and away from frosts.

6

Still he could not help comparing the army to that of Xerxes, the army, the caravan several leagues long and which carried with it so many wagons and so many luxurious carriages. He himself possessed a splendid brougham, quite new and laden with sugar, tea, furs and rare books.

But the battle of Malo-Iaroslavets robbed him of hope; he realized at once that the action fought between one only corps forming the advance-guard and the Russian army, must end disastrously and bring grievous consequences; and that the retreat, in altering its direction, must be made through a country already scoured and drained.[6]

As a matter of fact, the army returned through Mojaisk and re-crossed the field of the battle of the Moskova, and Boulart's

---

6. It was, Lejeune says, casting us back into the desert and amongst the ashes.

heart ached when he saw that spot of desolation and horror once again.

Up to November 6 the weather, though cool and damp, was still bearable and supplies did not fail. While the rear-guard was fighting, the rest of the army went quietly forward in a single column; but marching at ease became habitual and the number of stragglers increased.

On November 6 snow fell, covering the road, and then began the misery which was to increase day by day for six weeks.

Boulart describes it all—the wind lashing one's face; the snow hardened by the trampling of feet till it becomes ice; the holes and ditches into which those who strayed to right or left of the beaten track fall and disappear; the awful cold; the men who fall and whom no one lifts up; whose comrades, without a pause, without a look, leave to claw at the snow and struggle vainly against death.

He describes the life of the fugitives. During the day they march without a halt for fear of the Cossacks, breakfasting on a bit of bread or biscuit or sugar; biscuit and sugar, dry and hard as stones, breaking the teeth and laying bare the gums.

In the evening, near some village, eight or ten of them crowd close together round a bivouac-fire; they eat a wretched soup made of flour mixed with snow-water, then sleep, and the next day the march begins again.

"Since we left Moscow," sighed Berthier, "we have never ceased marching"; and the soldiers grumbled at this "pig-tail" which grew even longer and longer and seemed to have no end.

The garb of all these men, like their aspect, has something savage about it. Sunken eyes; beards grown thick; long moustaches; dirty and smoke-dried skins; they wear pelisses and furred great-coats of all shapes and colours, and are shod with rags, scraps of cloth or fur, more or less badly tied on with string.

On November 13, at Smolensk, there came a sort of lull in the storm.

On that day, when supplies were dealt out to the Guard,

Boulart had ranged his guns near one of the gates of the town, on a sort of promenade where the trees sheltered them from the snow.

He had received bread, biscuits and a big joint of meat, which the clever Jarlot dressed, and round his bivouac fire he gathered together and regaled some of his friends, among others, Colonel Griois.

While he lived Griois never forgot the repast given him by Boulart. The cold was intense—27 degrees—and the wine had to be broken up with a hatchet and melted at the fire; but Griois thought it a feast.

The next day but one, November 15, as a contrast and a sort of make-weight, was for Boulart the hardest day of the retreat.

Harassed by the Cossacks, he, with his guns, was due at Krasnoï. It was evening.

He comes to a narrow pass obstructed by vehicles of every kind, and for three hours, which he uses in feeding men and horses, he halts.

But there is no giving way of the obstruction, and the major is assured that to get through it is absolutely impossible.

Boulart does not hesitate; to wait longer would be fatal, laying himself open to falling into the hands of the Russians.

He issues orders that his carriages are to follow close upon one another, without a stop, and boldly, pitilessly, he makes his way through the confused mass of wagons; he pushes aside, he knocks down, any who bar his passage; he breaks and crushes everything in his way, giving no ear to cries and groans; he comes out upon an open road, rigid with ice; he has earth taken from the sides of the road and spread over the ground; one by one the gun-carriages are hoisted up to the top of the ascent, and, at last, at dawn, he reaches Krasnoï.

He acknowledges that he had to display energy and a determined will to overcome the difficulty, but he had thought the matter out.

After him, no one cleared the pass; the Russians took up their position on the height and seized the equipages through which

Boulart had so determinedly cloven his way.

He had other troublous moments. During the engagement at Krasnoï, he had to sacrifice part of his baggage; to throw cannon and ammunition into a lake; to burn gun-carriages and wagons. To get out of Krasnoï he had to leave one of his guns to the Cossacks.

Before reaching Liady, he had to cover Davout's retreat, and he envied the lot of the foot-soldiers, and well-nigh cursed his branch of the service, so painful and tiring it was.

At Orcha, on November 19, he was able to rest, and the Russians did not trouble this respite.

The French were already recovering their spirits; hope was born again in them, and, on the 20th, as they marched on Borissov, they believed better days were coming.

"Good God!" exclaims Boulart; "how we were trapped!"

It was learnt that Tchitchagov, holding Borissov, stopped the passage of the Beresina, and that, on the right of the army, Wittgenstein was advancing.

It was then that Berthier made the appalling speech heard by Dedem: "We are cut off on every side!"

And Boulart writes in the same strain: "We are hemmed in; it is a terrible situation, and consternation reigns on all sides."

But he adds that they did not quite despair, and that the confidence of the army in the Emperor was prodigious.[7]

The Beresina is crossed, Tchitchagov repulsed; the lengthy highway to Zembin travelled over, and they are on the road to Vilna.

Alas! the cold becomes more and more cruel. On December 8, Boulart, sleeping in a church where men are dying by scores, is awakened by a sinister and terrible cry, which makes him shudder: "Fly! fly! Everyone is dying here!"

---

7. "The sight of the Emperor reassured the army," writes Ségur. "For long it had been accustomed to rely on him, not for life but for conquest. This was the first unlucky campaign, and there had been so many lucky ones. All there was to do was to follow him; he alone, who had been able to raise his soldiers so high and so to dash them down, could save them! He lived in the midst of his army as hope fives in the heart of man!"

On the 9th, a couple of leagues from Vilna, in a farrier's shop without window or door and open to all the winds of heaven, with seven others, he crouches at a wretched little fire, his toes almost in the flames, and without a morsel to eat!

At last, on the 10th, he reaches Vilna, satisfies his hunger and sleeps in a good bed.

Suddenly he is snatched from sleep: Vilna can't be held; it must be left; and our gallant Major departs. He gets into an open carriage with Colonel Lallemand and Captain Evain, arrives at Kovno, and, on the 19th, he is at Gumbinnen, on Prussian soil.

7

On February 12, 1813, he once more saw his wife and children, whom he had left eleven months earlier. What events had taken place since then! The journey across Germany; the passage of the Niemen; the storm-deluge that had overtaken the army on its march to Vilna; the taking of Smolensk; the battle of the Moskova; the disaster at Krasnoï; the Beresina; "the most disastrous, the most awful retreat the world had ever seen!"

"After that," ends Boulart, "you can fancy what happiness I felt to be in the midst of all I hold most dear!"

But he was amongst the bravest of the year 1812; never allowing himself to be discouraged and never, for a moment, giving way to weakness.

Colonel Fezensac

1

Son-in-law of the Duc de Feltre, and with the rank of major, Fezensac[1] easily got permission to join the Russian Campaign.

Berthier, Major-General of the Grand Army, took him as his *aide-de-camp*, and at the beginning of the month of May, 1812, Fezensac went to Posen.

He crossed Prussia, remarking on his way the discontent of the people oppressed by billeting and requisitions. Not only had the peasants to feed their lodgers, they had to furnish the regiments with carts and horses and frequently take them fifty leagues from their villages, where, sick of war, they ended by leaving them.

But what mattered the complaints of the Prussians?

The Grand Army was on the march, certain of victory.

And what immense preparations! Each general possessed several carriages, and every officer had his. The number of servants, horses and baggage of all sorts was prodigious.

Officials abounded, and when Berthier reviewed the civil servants, from a distance they looked like troops drawn up in battle array.

---

1. Raymond, Viscount, then Due de Montesquiou-Fezensac, Brigadier-General, March 4, 1813; Lt.-General, July 30, 1823. In 1849 he published first a part of his *Journal de la Campagne de Russie*, then the whole of his military recollections from the time of his entering the Service in 1804 to the end of the Empire. In his *Souvenirs Militaires*, in three volumes, the second, consisting of ten chapters, is devoted to the Russian Campaign, and it is that alone we consider here.

And what an imposing mass of infantry, cavalry and artillery! And was not the quality as fine as the quantity?

At the beginning of the campaign, Fezensac was often sent with messages to the generals, and each time he extols the bearing of the regiments, their enthusiasm, the order and precision of their evolutions.

These regiments had only to appear; the Niemen was crossed without difficulty, Vilna entered without resistance. In a trice, the Emperor separated the two Russian armies and drove them before him. He made Vilna his headquarters and kindled the zeal of the Poles. Fezensac was present at the proclamation of the independence of Poland in the cathedral of the town; the men, dressed in the ancient costume, and the women, wearing ribbons of the national colours—red and purple—heard the act with acclamations.

But how great the difference between Poland and Prussia! In Prussia, comfort, well-cultivated land, well-built houses. In Poland, poverty and servitude; a sottish peasantry, horribly dirty Jews, fields scarcely cleared, noisome huts.

The resources of the country were not sufficient for the army, already in want of supplies; the stragglers and loiterers, whose number increased day by day, gave themselves up to pillage, and the *sous-préfet* of Novo-Troki, on his way to his post, arrived at the town he was to manage almost naked; our soldiers had robbed him!

The weather was unfavourable, at times stifling heat, at others torrents of rain which spoiled the roads, often consisting of nothing but long pieces of wood thrown over swamps.

Ten thousand horses perished in a few days.

2

Napoleon quits Vilna on June 16 and drives the Russians to the gates of Vitebsk. A great battle is expected; the regiments are afire with eagerness; their behaviour in several fights, and notably at Ostrovno, presages success; but the enemy falls back upon Smolensk.

There is a rest of a few days at Vitebsk—from June 29 to July 12—and Fezensac and his fellow-officers congratulate themselves on this fine beginning: Lithuania won, the Russians retaining no portion of it; and the genius of the Emperor, the skill of his generals, the valour of his soldiers, unite in giving hopes of a coming victory to be called the victory of Smolensk.

Still, some of the officers do not conceal their anxiety.

The French army is reduced by a third; the cavalry have lost a number of horses; the artillery gets on not without difficulty; the ambulance-convoys and the baggage-wagons with medicaments are still in the rear. The Russians, on the other hand, are retiring in admirable order, leaving behind not a single gun, a single carriage, a single sick man.

On August 16 these ever-retreating Russians are come up with before Smolensk, and they defend the town. On the 17th the attack is begun, the outskirts taken; and the assault would have taken place the same day if the wall the batteries attempted to breach had not been of a thickness that recalled that of the ramparts of Saint-Jean-d'Acre to the officers who had served with the Army of Egypt.

But in the night the Russians evacuated and set fire to Smolensk, leaving their wounded to perish in the flames and the inhabitants to huddle into the cathedral, where they died of hunger.

On the 19th they were pursued, caught up with at Valoutina, and beaten; and the 3rd corps, under Ney, displayed on that day so splendid a courage that the enemy believed itself faced by the Imperial Guard.

Still the victory was incomplete; no prisoners were taken, and the enemy, as usual, retired in perfect order to take up another position further on.

Fezensac thought it would have been better to halt between the Dwina and the Dnieper; to restore order to Lithuania and repair the losses of the army. But the Emperor was convinced that a decisive battle would lead to peace; and to secure that battle, he marched to Moscow. On September 1 he heard that

Koutouzov was resolutely awaiting him, and, truly, says Fezensac, never was news more welcome.

Napoleon had got his battle at last, and, on the 7th, when it came off, he refused to manoeuvre to the right so as to turn the Russians' left wing; he would have the battle at whatever cost and dreaded to let it escape him.

But Fezensac seems to regret that he took no personal part in the action and did not order the Guard to make the victory complete.

3

On September 11 Berthier's *aide-de-camp* was made colonel of the 4th regiment of the line. He was twenty-six years old!

From the earliest days of his command he is struck by the look of exhaustion of the troops and their numerical weakness. The 4th regiment used to have a strength of 2,800 men; now it has but 900 and forms two battalions instead of four. The 3rd corps, to which he belongs—Marshal Ney's Corps—formerly numbered 25,000 combatants and now counts but 8,000.

The effect on men's spirits of these very serious losses is evident; there is no more gaiety, no more songs or funny stories; the men keep a gloomy silence and the officers serve now only from a sense of duty and honour.

The burning of Moscow makes the gloom complete. Fezensac's regiment is encamped three-quarters of a mile behind the town, which it is expressly forbidden to enter; and if its young colonel tacitly allows his men to go in and take their share in the pillaging, they get no good out of the permission; for when they return with their booty, their kind comrades of the 1st Corps and of the Imperial Guard relieve them of the whole of it.

Later on, the 3rd corps is quartered in a suburb of Moscow, and the 4th regiment crosses the town to the beat of drums and the sound of martial music; but past what a scene of misery does this triumphal march roll on!

The air is filled with a horrible , smell of burning; rubbish of all sorts obstructs the way; the houses look as if they had been razed to the ground, and those still left standing are nothing but smoke-blackened walls.

Here and there a cottage, a house or a church rises above the wreckage. The inhabitants wander like spectres amongst the ruins, living on the vegetables still to be found in the gardens, the flesh of the horses fallen in the streets, or the fermented wheat fished out of the river into which the Russian army has cast it.

Fezensac's regiment is little better off; sugar and vegetables and preserves it has, but little meat and little bread. It possesses furs, but neither clothes nor shoes; it has diamonds, jewellery, ornaments, but it is on the eve of dying of hunger. Troops of auxiliaries already surround Moscow; Cossacks attack the foragers; peasants massacre the marauders.

Thus a month goes by.

On October 18 Napoleon reviews the 3rd corps in the court of the Kremlin. The regiments are in splendid case, and perhaps, says Fezensac, their appearance made the Emperor believe that with such troops nothing was impossible to him.

Then suddenly Berenger, Murat's *aide-de-camp*, makes his appearance and tells Napoleon of the repulse at Taroutino.

The Emperor cannot conceal his emotion; he hurries on the review, and gives the colonel the order to leave next day.

On October 19 they start. Fezensac leaves the flour he can't carry with him to the people of the house he has lived in, and the blessings they shower upon him brought him luck, he thinks.

4

This departure, which took place at night, had something lugubrious and sinister about it; the darkness, the silent march, the still smoking ruins beneath their feet, all awoke feelings of sadness and anxiety.

But during the last days of October Fezensac had nothing but praise to give to all his men.

On the way to Kalouga they were exposed to torrential rains, and their march was by absolutely broken crossroads. As they retraced their steps to Mojaisk they had to go by roads blocked with vehicles and over streams that had overflowed their banks. But the order and discipline of the 4th regiment never failed.

In November, after the affair at Viasma, its worst trials began. Up to then, fatigue and hunger were all it had had to contend with; now it was to struggle, as Fezensac says, against Death in every form, while covering with the 3rd corps the retreat of the army.

On the evening of the 5th of November, in the defile of Semlevo, Fezensac, unaided, keeps in check the Russian vanguard.

On the 8th, he defends Dorogobouge. Razout's division, shut up in the castle, is nearly surrounded; Fezensac with his regiment charges up the snow-covered heights, where they scatter and skirmish.

The Russians fall back, and when they renew their attack and Razout orders a return, it is Fezensac again who repulses them.

Ney is displeased.

"What were the enemies' numbers?" he asks Fezensac.

"We were too close to them for me to count," answers the colonel.

But the marshal was right in holding that the enemy had seized Dorogobouge too soon, and when General Joubert described to him the weakness and discouragement of the troops:

"The only question is to get oneself killed," replied Ney; "and such a death is too fine, too glorious to shun!"

All day on the 11th, while Ney was falling back on Slob-Pnévo, Fezensac guarded the road leading to the bridge over the Dnieper, and then the blockhouse on the opposite bank, he himself, with Ney, firing on the assailants.

On the evening of the 13th, not without trouble and difficulty, he encamped before Smolensk. But the 3rd corps was the last to arrive, and it found nothing left in the place; the corps that had preceded it had broken up and plundered the storehouses; it had taken no more than twenty-four hours to destroy the supplies for several months.

On the 15th, on the outskirts of Smolensk, amid snow and litter, Fezensac drove off the Russian sharpshooters and prevented them holding the head of the bridge.

From the top of a rampart, Ney watched the fight. He sent word to Fezensac not to advance too far, and the colonel remarks that such an order from the marshal was very rare.

On the 17th, in accordance with the Emperor's instructions, the 3rd corps left Smolensk, after blowing up the fortifications; and on the 18th on the march to Krasnoï, it found itself surrounded.

An envoy summoned Ney to lay down his arms; Ney's only answer was an order to attack the enemy. Fezensac led the way; but grape-shot overwhelmed his regiment, set on by both infantry and cavalry. In a quarter of an hour the 4th lost three-fifths of its strength.

We know how Ney saved what remained of the 3rd corps, and how he reached Orcha by the right bank of the Dnieper so quickly as to rejoin the Grand Army, which was moving along the left.

Fezensac distinguished himself during this fine retreat. For a moment he was cut off from the column, and the Cossacks, firing at him point-blank, assailed him in a wood. But he kept his presence of mind and maintained order amongst the men still left him. Bravely they followed him through the midst of the wood, then outside it along the Dnieper, over difficult ground, by. rugged ravines and half-frozen streams.

5

When Fezensac reached Orcha, the 3rd corps numbered only 800 men, and the regiment only eighty. When on November 27, after crossing the Beresina, the roll was called, out of seventy officers but forty were left, and most of these were sick and worn out; as to the men they made up two half companies.

The 3rd corps and its regiments had ceased to exist.

Ney decided that the officers with the flags should join the Imperial Guard, and the sound men, making a hundred, should remain with him as an escort.

Fezensac and the officers departed, a drummer at their head—the sole survivor of the drummers and bandsmen of the 3rd corps—and, after a march of two days and three nights, they came up with headquarters on December 3, between Iliya and Molodetchno, in a forest of pines.

Napoleon was in a carriage with Berthier, the *aides-de-camp* leading their horses by the bridle, and sometimes sitting behind the carriage to rest themselves [8]; the Guard walked in some kind of order, and after it came footsore men from every regiment.

Arrived at Vilna in the midst of crowding and confusion that recalled the Passage of the Beresina, struggling to suffocation with the crowd at the gates, the officers dispersed.

But on the 9th of December, having supped on a pot of jam and slept upon a board, Fezensac once more found his regiment, the regiment he regretted to have left; so true is it, he says, that in war one always repents having left one's post, even by order of one's chiefs, even with the intention of doing right.

He left Vilna with what was still left of the officers and men of the 4th regiment of the line; and, if he lost them while climbing the hill of Ponari, he joined them again further on at Chichmori and led them to Kovno: twenty officers and twenty men, of whom not one was fit to fight!

But he was tired to death, and while his men went to look for rum and biscuits, he let himself drop against a milestone in Kovno.

Yet, when Ney—Ney the rear-guard, as he might well have been called—ordered that this handful of men should remain with him to defend the place, neither Fezensac nor his companions replied that they had done enough and their task was ended.

Fezensac's pages concerning the taking of Kovno contain heartbreaking details.

---

8. Castellane says, in fact: "We walked and sat by turns, and nothing was a greater proof of our misery than that great personages looked upon this as a piece of good luck."

French soldiers, sitting round bivouac fires in the streets, gaze indifferently at Fezensac and his friends as they pass; and when they are told that they will fall into the hands of the Cossacks, hang their heads, and without a word crowd round the fire. Already the inhabitants stare insolently at the Frenchmen, and one of them arms himself with a musket, which Fezensac snatches from him.

Men who have dragged themselves as far as the Niemen fall dead upon the bridge at the very moment when the end of their troubles is at hand.

But beyond the Niemen appear the Russians; they have crossed the river on the ice, blocking the way of the fugitives, and then Fezensac sees two of his officers, stricken with despair, turning back to Kovno to give themselves up as prisoners. In vain he implores them not to forsake the regiment; they have come to the end of their strength, a supreme effort is beyond their powers; weeping, they embrace their colonel and go back to the town.

For the last time Marshal Ney saves his companions in arms. Under cover of the darkness he descends the Niemen, and, turning to the left, takes a road through the woods that leads to Königsberg. All night and the next day the march goes on. "A white horse we rode bare-backed by turns was a great help to us," says Fezensac.

6

Such is Fezensac's story.

He blames the expedition—the most disastrous history records; it was colossal, superhuman and, in consequence, doomed to failure.

What was the use of the enormous commissariat the Grand Army dragged behind it? Despite the zeal and the ability of the Intendant-General Dumas, it was well-nigh useless from the very beginning of the campaign, and, in the end, became absolutely detrimental.

It is not enough to give orders; it is necessary that such orders should be carried out; and, "what with the rapidity of the movements, the concentration of troops in one spot, the bad state of the roads, and the difficulty of feeding the horses, how could it have been possible to serve out regular rations and to organize the hospital service properly?" Some of his criticisms on the men and officers are curious and instructive.

Some leagues from Vilna Fezensac meets with several regiments of the Young Guard, among others the regiment of "*Flanqueurs*" This regiment, since leaving Saint-Denis, has had but two days of rest, one at Mayenne and one at Marienwerder; moreover, after the day's march, it has to drill after reaching its quarters because the Emperor does not think it smart enough. Now this regiment is composed of very young men: "Therefore it was the first to go to pieces; already the men were dying of exhaustion on the roads."

He classes the officers of the regiment he commands as follows: some, fresh from the Military College, active, zealous, but too young and raw to endure the excessive hardships of the campaign; others, old non-commissioned officers, excellent soldiers, and who know everything the practice of warfare can teach in the lower grades, but wanting in intelligence and education; others, cultivated, experienced, hardy and anxious to distinguish themselves, but of whom, unluckily, there is but a small number.

He draws the portraits of the generals and colonels of his army corps—Ledru des Essarts, who has a marvellous knowledge of the details of the service; Razout, short-sighted, unable to distinguish anything about him, and always uncertain, irresolute and undecided; Joubert, of a commonplace kind; a'Hénin, who, long a prisoner in England, has lost the habit of his profession; Pelleport, who commands the 18th Regiment with rare distinction.

He praises both Mortier and Berthier.

Mortier, ordered to blow up the Kremlin, manages the task in a fashion that diminishes something of its severity, and his dealings with the sick and wounded and the care he takes of them do honour to his character and his heart.

Berthier treats his *aides-de-camp* roughly but kindly, and lets them want for nothing. He spends the day, and even the night, in despatching the Emperor's commands, and never were seen such obedience and such absolute devotion. Nevertheless, as recompense for his services, he gets nothing but rebuffs and severe reprimands; but his zeal never abates and his patience is untiring. Incapable of high command, he possesses in the highest degree the qualifications necessary for Napoleon's chief of staff.

Fezensac has less praise for Marshal Davout.

In one short sentence he alludes to the Prince d'Eckmühl, blaming him for his pitiless severity when, acting as rear-guard, he was ordered to set fire to everything: "Never was order carried out with more exactness and fewer scruples."

Our colonel speaks but little of Napoleon. He remarks that the Emperor visited the wounded after the battle of the Moskova, and gave orders that they were to be well looked after.

He notes his habit of smartly rating the supply and hospital officials, and in consequence the soldiers, dying of want, would blame no one but these same officials, saying: "It's very unfortunate; for the Emperor takes a great deal of trouble about us."

Finally, Fezensac describes a fit of anger of Napoleon's; one of those fits Napoleon called "my blood-red rages."

At Viasma, on August 30, seeing some men plundering a brandy-store, the Emperor rushes in amongst them, hurling abuse at them, and striking them with his riding-whip; and Fezensac gathers from this performance that the conqueror, exasperated at his failure to reach the Russians, who ravage and burn without granting him the battle he longs for, gave way to fits of ill-temper of which those around him were often the victims.

The hero of these recollections, the personage whose figure dominates this little volume and whose great personality claims both Fezensac's homage and ours, is Marshal Ney.

Hardened by experience of war, rough and harsh, but neither cruel nor malicious, Ney ended by holding that all soldiers ought to die on the field of battle, and so fulfil their destiny.

"Let me be carried off," a wounded man calls out to him. "Eh!" answers the marshal; "what do you want me to do about it? You are a victim of the war"; and he passes on.

Fezensac mourns the death of Alfred de Noailles. "Bah!" says Ney; "apparently it was his turn, and it is better for us to be regretting him than for him to be regretting us."

But he took no count of his own life, and his boldness, his steadfastness, his coolness, were so wonderful!

In Fezensac's eyes Ney was the best fitted for commanding the rear-guard. Ney ceded Dorogobouge to the Russians with great grief, lamenting his inability to hold it twenty-four hours longer.

At Slob-Pnévo, in the crossing of the Dnieper, his operations are exceedingly skilful. If he is present, the men's minds are at rest, however great the danger; they are ignorant of what he wants or is able to do; but they know he will do something.

"What have you decided to do?" says an officer to him on the evening of November 18.

"To cross the Dnieper."

"But how?"

"That we shall find out."

"And if the Dnieper is not frozen?"

"It will be frozen."

Thereupon the marshal catches sight of ice and orders it to be broken; it is a stream flowing into the Dnieper. He follows this stream and reaches a village, where he makes as if to take up his quarters.

The village is deserted, but at last a lame peasant is found who guides the troops to the Dnieper. The river is frozen; they cross it, leaving guns, baggage and carriages to the enemy.

The next day they fight all day with the Cossacks and rest in the evening. At one o'clock in the morning they start again and march till dawn; once more they repulse the Cossacks, from noon till fall of day defending a village backed by a wood, and in the night they come to within a league of Orcha.

The confidence inspired by the Duc d'Elchingen and his un-alterable coolness in danger have saved the remnant of the 3rd corps, and a week later, on November 28, on the right bank of the Beresina, when he succeeds to the command of the wound-ed Oudinot, it is he that brings about the success of the battle.

From the 9th to the 13th of December, at Vilna and at Ko-vno, it is he, the stubborn soldier, who makes the army's last stand against the Russians; "his absence," says Fezensac, "would have meant total loss and his presence redeemed everything."

7

But the finest portrait in these memoirs is that of Fezensac, drawn by himself unwittingly in scattered touches.

The reader feels the liveliest sympathy for the colonel, and applauds the justice of the praises the Duc d'Elchingen bestowed on him after the campaign.

On January 23, 1813, Marshal Ney wrote to the Duc de Fel-tre: "I want to express to you the great satisfaction I feel in the way M. de Fezensac behaved. That young man found himself in very critical situations, and always showed himself superior to them. I present him to you as a true French knight, and for the future you can look upon him as a colonel of old standing."

Fezensac is full of courage and resolution. After Vilna, he de-clares that the stragglers, the wretches who, still sound of limb, desert their corps, ought to be driven off at the butt-end of the musket; and, should the enemy make an attack, he threatens to fire on them if they cause the slightest difficulty.

He holds that these stragglers, no longer belonging to any regiment or serving in any way, have no right to be pitied; and he allows his own men, soldiers loyal to the colours and, as rear-guard, alone in their resistance to the enemy, to take from these stragglers their food and clothing.

"We were reduced to destroying each other; but it was an unavoidable necessity."

At Dorogobouge, as soon as Razout orders an advance,

Fezensac instantly attacks the Russians, and when Razout orders the retreat, the order has to be repeated before he quits his position; and he draws back slowly, forming his company anew and still facing the enemy.

Energetically he recalls his men to their duty, and on November 14 when, outside Smolensk, they take refuge in the houses to shelter from the terrible cold, he tells them that their honour is at stake, and that to disperse is to expose themselves to a surprise, and so compromise their division and the entire army. He exhorts them to carry out the noble task entrusted to them by Ney, and so always to deserve the marshal's praise.

He is proud of the fame they have won with him and under his command.

A generous emotion fills his heart when he describes to us how, at Krasnoï, his men walked calmly into the jaws of death. "Let me pay homage to their devotion," he writes, "and congratulate myself on having marched at their head."

How proudly he tells us how his officers rivalled each other in enthusiasm at the fight on the outskirts of Smolensk; how sorrowfully he recalls the destruction of his regiment—his "family"—at Krasnoï!

He owns that his courage failed him when his friends and comrades fell before his eyes; he loved them with all his heart; he shared with them, and they shared with him, their last morsel of bread; for, he says, " authority was paternal in those days and subordination founded on attachment and confidence; the colonels inspired respect, and the only way to alleviate the many troubles was united life, mutual help and service."

Moreover, Fezensac refused to leave the remnant of his regiment; he wanted to animate, to stimulate it to the end by his example. On December 12, between Chichmori and Kovno, though so worn out with fatigue that more than once he had well-nigh fallen by the way, he answered two officers who offered to take him on in their sledge with an energetic "no"; and he seconds the last efforts of Ney, whose heroic obstinacy he admires.

How touching and true is the epigraph he places at the head of his *Souvenirs*.

O, ashes of Ilion and shades of my companions, I call you to witness that, in your disaster, I recoiled neither before the darts of the enemy, nor before any kind of danger, and that if my destiny had so willed it, I was worthy to die with you.

Iliaci cineres et flamma extrema meorum,
Testor, in occasu vestro, nec tela, nec ullas
Vitavisse vices Danaum; et si fata fuissent
Ut caderem, meruisse manu.

8

Beside so many stories of the same kind, Fezensac's is still worthy of our attention and respect.

With strict but poignant brevity he narrates the march from Krasnoï to Orcha, when Ney's corps, cut off from the army, found no hope but in despair; that unequal fight, the finest of the campaign, in which the ability of the general and the devotion of the troops shone with unsurpassed brilliancy.

He depicts the irresistible growth of disorder as soon as it takes hold of a large army.

He describes the retreat as it really was: the route and the bivouacs looking like a battlefield; those who could stand the cold, sinking under fatigue; those who could stand fatigue and cold succumbing to the torments of hunger; those who had kept a little food, too weak to follow the column and falling into the hands of the enemy; some frozen to death upon the ice; others, asleep in the villages, perishing in the flames lighted by their companions; others distracted, like the soldier who reels all of a sudden, and, wild-eyed, inquires of his companions what has become of his regiment; those who managed to escape, living miraculously on soaked flour, a little honey or horse-flesh, exhausted, sick, stumbling at every step and with no strength left to carry a gun; struggling over melancholy wastes covered with snow as far as the eye could reach; through great forests of pines and past burnt-out villages; black with dirt and smoke;

shod with sheep-skin or bits of cloth; heads bound with rags; wrapped in horse-cloths or women's petticoats; and as soon as one falls never to rise again, stripping him of his rags even before he dies.

In Fezensac's *Souvenirs* there is more than one striking and touching passage.

On the night of November 16, on the eve of quitting Smolensk, Fezensac goes about the town, now nothing but a heap of ruins. Some houses are still left standing, but their doors and windows are broken, and their chambers heaped with corpses; on the pavements lie the skeletons of horses, whose flesh has been devoured, in their common distress, by soldiers and inhabitants alike; and Fezensac never forgot the melancholy he felt in those deserted streets; in the glow of the fires reflected on the snow, a strange contrast with the soft radiance of the moon.

Here is a picture of Vilna as it appeared on December 9.

Up to that time the French have seen nothing but towns burnt or abandoned by their inhabitants, and Nature smitten, as it were, by a Divine malediction.

But Vilna is untouched, presenting the aspect of a wealthy and populous town, its people busy each at his special work.

Suddenly our soldiers flock in, wandering about the streets in rags and dying of hunger; some paying its weight in gold for wretched food, others begging for a morsel of bread.

The inhabitants regard them with a diversity of sentiments— the Poles with grief, the Russians with joy, the Jews with the hope of making much out of them.

Then they begin to be afraid; they dread a famine; they close shops, inns, cafés; they hide their provisions.

Soon comes the noise of cannon; uproar everywhere; the fire-bell rings out; a few of the braver spirits hasten to the gates to repel the enemy; the others, resting either on the pavements or in houses where they are on sufferance, declare they can do no more and will stop where they are.

Shall we quote the passages in which Fezensac tells how the days of plenty followed those of want?

The fugitives are in Prussia. The Jews, who believe the Frenchmen to be loaded with treasures, sell to them the commonest of garments at the highest prices. The Prussians, without concealment of their hatred, question them with malicious curiosity, pity them ironically, give them false news of the approach of the Cossacks, and at times disarm, threaten and ill-treat them. A Protestant minister tells Fezensac that God has justly punished the Grand Army.

But the French care little for this unpleasant reception; the joy of finding food and sleeping in a warm room makes up to them for everything. Königsberg, in spite of the excessive insolence of its inhabitants, seems to them a land flowing with milk and honey; the cafés and shops are never empty; the officers spend their nights at table; the men traffic in jewellery and other valuables they have brought from Russia; and in a short time "all the money in the town is carried off."

Anecdotes—often incredible anecdotes—abound in these *Memoirs*. Some of them are horrible.

At Moscow, a French officer discovers a Russian hiding amongst the ruins of a house; by signs he makes him understand that he will protect him, takes him with him and hands him over to a passing comrade, saying; "I give you *Monsieur* in charge"; and the other officer, mistaking the sense of the words, takes the poor wretch for an incendiary and forthwith has him shot.

During the retreat, a general, worn out with fatigue, drops down on the road, and a soldier begins to pull off his boots.

"Wait anyhow till I'm dead," says the general, as he tries to sit up

The man answers; "*Mon General*, I wish I could; but someone else will take them, and it may just as well be me."

A soldier is stripping a dying man. "Let me, do let me die in peace," says the last.

"I beg your pardon, comrade," replies the other; "I thought you were dead."

And this cruel egoism is sometimes accompanied by a hideous irony.

Two soldiers hear an officer lying on the snow calling to them for help, saying he is an officer of engineers.

"What, an officer of Engineers!"

"Yes, my man."

"Well, then, draw out your plan!"

But Fezensac tells some touching stories too.

The wife of a drummer of the 7th Light Infantry, the *cantinière* of the same regiment, falls ill at the beginning of the retreat. The man drives her as long as he has a cart and horse; at Smolensk the horse dies and the man harnesses himself to the cart and draws his wife to Vilna. Once there, he is too weak to go further, and he stays with her as a prisoner.

A *cantinière* of the 33rd regiment of Infantry gives birth to a child in Prussia before the commencement of the campaign, and accompanies the regiment with her little girl, who is six months old when the army leaves Moscow.

The child was saved; her mother fed her on nothing but black-puddings made with horses' blood; she had wrapped her up in furs taken at Moscow; twice she lost her and twice found her again, the first time in a field, the second on a mattress in a burnt-out village.

When the Beresina had to be passed, she crossed the river on horseback, holding the reins with one hand while with the other she held the little girl seated on her head.

Thus, by a series of miracles, this child went through the retreat without even catching cold.

And did not Bourgoyne see soldiers for days together carrying a wounded officer on their shoulders? Was not General Legrand carried by his grenadiers; General Zayonchek by his Poles; Colonel Marin by his gunners; young Sainte-Croix by his friends?

For the comfort of humanity, says Fezensac, many an act of sublime devotion contrasted there with the many others dictated by selfishness and inhumanity.

Guillaume Peyrusse

1

Appointed paymaster of the Royal Treasury during the Russian expedition, with a monthly stipend of 940 *francs* and a daily indemnity of twelve *francs*, and bound to accompany everywhere the two wagons containing the funds which always followed the Emperor's carriages, Guillaume Peyrusse started on the night of March 5, 1812. He carried with him twelve millions in gold, and five chests of jewels.

Whither was he bound? First of all to Dresden; it was there that Napoleon had asked the Emperor of Austria to meet him, and where there was to be a sort of assembly of princes.

But after that? He hardly knew. Even at Mayenne, even at Posen, he is ignorant of the goal of what he calls the trip. He saw many troops, regiments of workmen of all sorts and battalions of oxen; he saw fine carriages and immense preparations.

But nothing proclaimed war, and everybody, as we read in one of Peyrusse's letters,[1] invented his fable, knew his bit of gossip, made up stories of every kind.

"Do they want to found a colony," he exclaims, "where I should make the first of a branch of paymasters?"

But, at bottom, it mattered little to him. The Emperor's plans were impenetrable and "His Majesty seems to be very mysterious concerning his progress." Well, as for Peyrusse himself, he must go wherever Napoleon goes, were it to Constantinople,

---

1. *Lettres de Peyrusse*, published by L. G. Pelissier, pp. 52-132.

or Egypt, or India; were it to the ends of the earth. Hadn't he got a comfortable carriage and two good horses; *fourgons* full of provisions that he wouldn't begin upon till the last moment, and excellent health?

At Mayenne he had dined with the Comptroller General Reiset and the Préfet Jeanbon Saint-Andre; at Frankfort he dined with the great banker Gontard, in the company of diplomats and *foireux*—that is to say, wealthy merchants who had come to the fair—and he gives an interesting description of the repast.

Dish after dish; a profusion of German wine not worth one bottle of Burgundy; the German excess of politeness; men bowing to you incessantly, taking your hands and appearing to love you as themselves; servants greedy for tips, and who "must be bold beggars to stand in front of you as you come out from dinner, almost holding out their hands to you."

At last, after having seen at Fulde the palace of the Prince-Bishop; at Wartburg, the room, the table and the inkstand of Luther; at Leipzig the fair, which seemed to him to be a picture in little of all Europe; and at Meissen, the porcelain factory; and after having spent eight days in Dresden, the Paymaster Peyrusse travelled towards Posen.

In the month of May he was in Poland, and he uttered a cry of horror. "What wretched villages—what disgusting dirtiness!"

Certainly each village had its castle; but what was this castle but just a house larger than the other houses, and as neglected and ill-kept as the rest?

It was at Posen that he realized—it had taken him some time—that Napoleon proposed to invade Russia.

But rumours of peace were in the air; some people believed that the Emperor's stay in Dresden, his brilliant surroundings and the threatening aspect of the Grand Army would decide Alexander to come to terms.[2]

---

2. Sergeant Lebas, of the 33rd regiment of Foot, wrote from Dantzig to his family on April 23: "Many of the townspeople tell me every day that they are well assured the Emperor of Russia does not want to fight." 1812, *La guerre de Russie, notes et documents,* passim.

"That will be as the Emperor wishes," repeats Peyrusse; "the longer the journey he causes me to make, the better pleased I am. I travel very comfortably; I receive the consideration due to me, and all this moving about amuses me immensely."

2

But soon there is no more doubt about war. Peyrusse sees the Emperor arrive at Königsberg and make every preparation for his great adventure.

They were "off like a shot," even before a postal service could be inaugurated.

"The Emperor has never been more calm and energetic," writes Peyrusse to his brother; "but I don't know where he intends taking us; he is leading us a pretty dance."

They cross the Niemen and push on towards Vilna.

"A lively resistance was expected," says Peyrusse, "but nothing happened but a little sword-play—no serious engagement; the Russians haven't made up their minds to bite yet; but the two giants will end by meeting one of these days; they will come into collision, and the earth will tremble under the tremendous shock."

He describes the kind of welcome Vilna gave the Emperor; the organization of the Government of Lithuania, and the attitude of Napoleon, who, when a deputation from the Confederation begs him to re-establish the Kingdom of Poland, answers with great reserve and caution.[3]

The army leaves Vilna and pursues its way past Gloubokoïé and Kamen, and over a sterile country where nothing is to be seen but wretched scattered villages, inhabited, says Peyrusse, by a sort of animals with nothing human about them but their faces.

But our paymaster keeps his cheerfulness; he has taken every precaution; he has supplies. When he bivouacs in the midst of

---

3. M. de Pradt puts it better than Peyrusse: "Napoleon's answer was involved and evasive."

a forest he drinks good wine and eats good biscuit with a savoury salad; he sleeps in a wagon on bear-skins, which serve him for a bed; so he stands the journey very well. He crosses the Plain of Ostrovno, where Murat and the Army of Italy distinguished themselves by fine feats of arms, and, on July 28, he enters Vitebsk.

3

At Vitebsk there is a halt—a long halt—and Peyrusse is happy. For the last two months he has seen nothing but solitude and ruins, and therefore Vitebsk wears the most smiling aspect for him, and his eyes rest with pleasure on a clean and even fashionable town.

For the easier reviewing of his troops, the Emperor has had several houses in the square in front of the palace pulled down. There are parades like those at the Tuileries; one might believe oneself living in a time of peace.

Peyrusse and his friends concoct schemes; they reconstruct the kingdom of Poland, giving it Riga and the Dnieper as boundaries; they take from Russia its Turkish provinces to hand them over to Austria or to give them back to the Sultan; they are of opinion that the appalling growth of the Muscovite Empire must be stopped, and they have absolute confidence in Napoleon. By his tactics he has baffled the Russians, and he will not fail to bend them to his will.

The march recommences on August 11; the Dnieper, which is no longer the Borysthenis of the Greeks, is crossed; they pass through Liady and Krasnoï and arrive under the walls of Smolensk.

But the enemy evacuates the town after making a desperate defence. Peyrusse sees there a "horrible devastation"; everywhere houses still burning; squares and churches filled with dead and dying; a few pale and hopeless inhabitants amongst the ruins.

Again the victors move onwards; leaving behind them Dorogobouge and Viasma— pretty Viasma, lying on the plain where the river of the same name makes pleasant twists and turns.

But Viasma, like Smolensk, is half destroyed, and accustomed as he has become to fires, Peyrusse casts a look of pity at its people.[4]

4

On September 3 they are at Ghiatsk; on the 5th the roar of cannon proclaims that the enemy has ceased retiring, and the wounded bring back word that it is

occupying all the heights, that it looks as if it was determined to hold its position, and that a redoubt covering its left wing has been taken by Compans's Division.

On the 7th the Battle of the Moskova is fought.

Peyrusse, from his post at the rear, hears the cannon "roaring furiously," and his hair stands on end; but at a quarter past three, he hears that the Emperor has pronounced these words: "In this way battles are won"; and he is reassured.

On the 8th he walks over the field of battle, and on the plain and in the ravines he sees nothing but the dead and the moaning wounded. The great redoubt is strewn with corpses.

There are few or no prisoners, no trophy to console the army for the cruel losses it has sustained. Once again the Russians have displayed an extraordinary stubbornness in fight; to kill them you had to knock them down, and so desperate were they, that in the already taken redoubt, in the thick of the fight, or even under the stockades, they went on firing.

The vanquished were pursued; Mojaisk taken. But again the enemy sets fire to the town, and Peyrusse's heart is torn when he sees the wounded Russians crawling along the streets and there, heaped on each other, uttering terrible cries at the sight of the flames eddying around them.

Besides, it is now only by the light of fires kindled by unseen hands that they advance, and Peyrusse begins to complain.

The bivouacs are no longer amusing; he dislikes sleeping in the open air; he has no more wine; he feels but middling well.

---

4. Fezensac, too, says: "We felt especial regret for the little town of Viasma, whose houses were devoured by the flames."

Luckily, Moscow is not far off—Moscow, the limit of the expedition, the end of pain and weariness. All hearts are full of joy and hope.

At noon, on September 14, when they reach the Holy Mountain, they see what looks a forest in the air—thousands of spires and belfries.

It is Moscow—holy Moscow—Moscow the Mother, the Russians, from this height, salute with prostrations and reverently making the sign of the cross!

At two o'clock, Peyrusse enters the town, and, as he says, the beauty, the immensity of Moscow, filled him with astonishment; wide streets; walls of various colours; gilded cupolas; magnificent houses; palaces "having a look of grandeur and wealth; how striking a variety!"

But already the shops have been broken into and given up to pillage; wine, brandy, liqueurs run about the streets. Soldiers pass with their booty, loaded with food, bottles, furniture.

About the squares, and on the bridges, in front of the churches and at the gates of the palaces, lie, or rather sprawl, *moujiks*, men belonging to the scum of the people, with evil countenances.

At last Peyrusse reaches the Kremlin. He takes possession of his quarters, and at once writes to his brother that he is very glad to have reached the goal.

In the action of the 7th the Russians could gauge our strength, "and must have guessed that the French army would play the devil to get here. It will get in unhindered and will soon be itself again."

5

That same evening the fire broke out; no fire-engine nor firemen to be had; the fire consumed two-thirds of Moscow. Chauffeurs, carrying torches and bags of gun-powder, were seized and shot or hung; but the Kremlin and the town itself had to be left.

Peyrusse's narrative here becomes very interesting.

The wagons, preceded and followed by a long train of vehicles, make a slow progress across Moscow, along streets blocked by pieces of furniture, and amidst burning beams falling from the houses; to the sound of the cries, or rather howls, of fright uttered by the drivers and coachmen, and surrounded by a mob of soldiers, who incessantly force their way into the palaces and shops, coming and going and carrying off provisions and goods of all kinds.

Peyrusse is forced to stop every few minutes; he is roasted in his carriage, and distressfully wonders if he will ever be able to save the Imperial Treasury and himself.

At the sight of a half-burnt bridge he will have to cross, he leaves the rank and attempts another passage; but the fire is all around him and has already reached the forage stored behind the wagons.

Fearing that he will be hemmed in by a labyrinth of flames, Peyrusse makes at full speed towards a bridge still whole at the beginning of the suburbs; he clears the bridge; clears the suburb past all sorts of obstacles; by a supreme effort clears the gate of the town, and with his horses at full gallop, reaches the castle of Petrovski.

Three days he stayed in that castle with its crenellated walls flanked by towers, like the roof, covered with varnished and many-coloured tiles. Thence he gazes sadly at the fire, bent like a rainbow over Moscow, agreeing with his companions in thinking that the entire city is given over to the flames; for did not successive reports tell that the scourge had reached hitherto safe districts, that the number of incendiaries was increasing, that Moscow was no longer habitable?

At last, on the 18th, the Emperor decided to go back to the Kremlin. The return to the town was made past the encampments set up to right and left of the road, and there Peyrusse witnessed what was called the Fair of Moscow.

Soldiers, black with mud and smoke, sitting in chairs of crimson velvet, eating soup from plates of porcelain and drinking from glasses of finest crystal. Others, dressed up in Tartar or Chinese costumes, feeding the bivouac fires with pieces of furniture, logs of mahogany or log-wood. Others publicly selling, dirt-cheap, all sorts of wares: sacks of flour and packets of cinnamon; clocks and candelabra; cloth and muslin; precious stuffs and cashmere shawls they had used to wrap ham or codfish in; and convicts and prostitutes mingling with them so as to share in the plunder and the sale.

6

Thus they returned to Moscow in the midst of the chests, the barrels, the rafters that littered the roads.

Peyrusse installed himself anew in the Kremlin, and he describes all he has seen, or half -seen of the town. The Kremlin, fortress and palace in one; the gigantic cross of St. Ivan, which Napoleon wished to place on the dome of the *Invalides*, and which was broken to pieces on the ground because the sappers who were ordered to remove it let it fall; the Bourse, or, as Peyrusse calls it, the *Palais Royal*, where millions of things had been burnt; the churches and their steeples; the palaces, and especially the Orlov Palace, where the elegance of the furniture matched the beauty of the gardens and park; the palace of the University, now used as barracks, and other lordly dwellings. Other magnificent houses, whose lower rooms had been turned into guard-houses and where the soldiers boil their saucepans on the drawing-room floors; the German quarter, where, in *fresco*-painted houses, live the greater number of the foreign artisans.

A month goes by; little by little they succeed in getting rid of the incendiaries, who, armed with tinder-boxes and tarred sticks, still go on setting fire to houses, even amongst the timbers of the roofs or under the boarding of the floors.

The flames have not destroyed all the supplies in the town; a considerable stock of provisions is found—there is such an abundance of coffee, tea and sugar, that they don't know what to do with it.

To the extreme surprise of the Russians, accustomed to snow from the early days of September, the weather is glorious, and the reviews held by the Emperor are all the more imposing.

But in Moscow not more than a tenth of its houses are left; on whatever side one turns one's eyes, there is nothing to be seen but "devastation and destruction." In certain quarters, the line of the streets can no longer be distinguished, and amidst heaps of cinders and ashes, stand the stone-built palaces, blackened by smoke, and looking, says Peyrusse, like ancient ruins.

Not an open shop, not a shop-keeper; not a laundress, not a tailor, not a shoemaker. Crowds wait round the French shoemakers; forage is rare, syrup and sweet-meats plentiful; so are lemons and liqueurs, but if one can cram oneself with these, there is little meat and little bread.

So wintering in Moscow is an impossibility.

Soon comes news that the peasants are arming; that Cossacks are attacking detachments and the convoys of artillery and provisions; sensible people no longer believe in peace.

After so violent and barbarous a deed as was the burning of Moscow; after so unprecedented an outrage, is it likely the Russians will come to terms with us? exclaims Peyrusse. Still, let them take heed—barbarians, cannibals that they are!

Peyrusse threatens them with reprisals.

Let them go on retiring, even to beyond the Volga; the French will pay them in their own coin! In the coming campaign they will burn St. Petersburg and overwhelm the port of Cronstadt!

7

On the 18th of October comes the shock of the news that the vanguard has been surprised and defeated at Taroutino; and on the morrow begins the retreat.

What an endless string of carts and carriages! It is several leagues in length, and never had Peyrusse, he says, seen such a crowd, such baggage, such a crush. The future, adds the paymaster, looks dark.

It was intended to take the road to Kalouga and march across new country; the battle of Malo-Iaroslavets had been won, the Russians driven back and their position taken at the point of the bayonet; but the action was too long drawn out and very bloody, and, despite the gallantry of the troops, who gave the enemy the full benefit of their strength, they had to face about and make their way back towards Mojaisk.

Once more they pass Borodino. Fragments of arms and cuirasses; stumps of guns; scraps of uniforms; skeletons of men and horses; corpses dug up and gnawed by dogs; graves covered with crosses, show plainly enough that this is the field of battle of September 17; and Peyrusse shudders as he looks once more at the great redoubt that dominates the plain, the redoubt whose conquest Caulaincourt had bought by his heroic death.

Already privations of all kinds have to be endured; no rations are served out; there is no way of relieving the sick and wounded they carry with them. In the rear the "hourras" of the Cossacks are heard from time to time.

And behold, on November 6, the heavens themselves turn against the French! The sun is hidden; the wind blows furiously; the snow falls in thick flakes; the cold comes, keen and penetrating.

The burnt-out villages offer no shelter; the gunners forsake their guns; soldiers lie dead by the dead fires of the bivouacs; others sink exhausted and never rise again.

There is hope of rest and food at Smolensk; but discipline and military bearing have gone; hunger, fatigue and sickness have demoralized the army. Wild with hunger, the soldiers rush into Smolensk; they slaughter the oxen, butcher the flocks; they break into and pillage the shops, an enormous quantity of provisions is scattered about and trodden under foot.

On November 12 Peyrusse leaves Smolensk, deploring, as he expresses it, the sad effects of the disorder, and through frost and snow, makes his difficult way to the Dnieper.

But the next day, the 13th, how many corpses he sees all along the road!

All the fallen men had thrown away their muskets; the touch of the iron on the bare hand was as painful as touching a live coal.

"This sight," says Peyrusse, "moved me strongly; I was not yet so miserable as to have lost all feeling."

What a night was that of the 14th!

In the distance he hears the cannon at Krasnoï, and in the village of Korytnia, in a wretched shed, by a fire that gives out more smoke than heat, he watches till morning, unable to sleep, in constant anxiety, keeping his servants on the alert, determined to die upon his coffer.

On the 15th, in the defile of Krasnoï, the way is barred by an immense number of equipages and guns; the Cossacks seize the front carriages; it is only by waiting and by favour of the darkness that the *fourgon* of the Imperial Treasury, with its escort of grenadiers, can force a way through the crowd.

At dawn of day, on the 16th, Peyrusse reaches Krasnoï by a steep incline, and over a road strewn with cartridges and debris of all kinds, full of spiked guns and horses swallowed up in mud.

He bivouacs on the village-green; everybody is dull and gloomy. As at Smolensk, the soldiers have pillaged the shops and lie down round fires fed with the woodwork of demolished houses.

On the 17th, an excessively cold morning, Napoleon, wearing a green pelisse, a cap on his head and a cane in his hand, comes out of his quarters. The Russians who outflank Krasnoï and intercept the road must be driven off; firing begins and lasts some long time; there is a rush to the road, which is speedily blocked by the crowd of stragglers and a number of vehicles. But the Cossacks, uttering fearful shouts, succeed in making a temporary gap. Soldiers and drivers make off in a fright. Peyrusse urges on his horses, upsets everything that gets in his way, and, at a gallop, reaches Liady.

It is at Liady that he spends the night between the 17th and 18th of November. The French are crowded together in this village, order and subordination no longer exist; the troops are all mixed up; the officers have ceased to command; so what can they henceforth expect of their subalterns?

Peyrusse departs under the protection of Claparéde's Division; but the 18th of November is again a cruel day, and the cold is excruciating. Luckily, Doubrovna is reached that evening, and there the Jews sell flour and mead to the fugitives.

The 19th again is icy cold, and there are ravines to cross; at every moment Peyrusse hears the sound of the powder-chests being blown up by the artillery, which has to leave them behind for want of horses—that sound that so profoundly grieved Eblé, Drouot, Griois and our brave gunners.

He reaches Orcha and the Dnieper. There, at the approach to the two bridges that have been constructed over the river, stand picked *gendarmes*, sent from France, who can't conceal their astonishment at the sight of this army in rags. But in vain do they endeavour to keep order and stop the stragglers. Some Cossacks appear, and the crowd of fugitives rushes tumultuously and unchecked to the further bank.

8

The situation becomes critical; Peyrusse sees carriages, papers belonging to the staff and the Emperor's Council-chamber burnt; he grows uneasy and alarmed. His well-horsed, well escorted *fourgon* inspires confidence and many officers of the Imperial household have handed over their savings to the paymaster. So he fears for his deposit; he can't sleep for thinking about it, and his excitement is so great that he does not feel the cold; every alarm, every pass makes his fears the worse; he is ashamed of himself.

But, in spite of the Emperor's proclamations and harangues, the confusion continues, and, on the 24th, the 25th, and the 26th of November, once more the thunder of cannon is heard afresh; the rumour spreads that the Bridge of Borissov is burnt, attacked from both banks of the Beresina; that the Russians have got the army between two fires; the Emperor is manoeuvring to outwit them.

By Bobr and Kroupki, our paymaster arrives, on the evening of the 26th, within view of Borissov, in a terrible wind which whips the snow into one's face, amongst a crowd of equipages, and pale-faced, jaded soldiers, wrapped in tattered pelisses or half-burnt sheepskins.

His *fourgon* falls into a ditch with slippery sides, and to get it out, it has to be unloaded.

But at dawn, on the 27th, on a height beside some houses, he catches sight of the light infantry of the Guard. It is Stoudienka, the headquarters—the palace, as Napoleon's dwelling, whether mansion or hovel, is called—and he hastens to reach it.

Here again is indescribable disorder, and Peyrusse, thinking of the decisive battle about to be fought; listening to the constant din of the guns and cries of the drivers; seeing the artillery-men striving to force a way through the crowd; Peyrusse feels more anxious, more troubled than ever.

At three o'clock in the afternoon he has orders to cross the bridge; at seven, he has not yet been able to get a place in the enormous and disorderly mass of vehicles.

But this time he knows no pity; too miserable, he says, to care, like a savage fighting for his own safety, he allows no one to break the rank.

At seven o'clock comes a frightful rush; Peyrusse's wagon is shot to the entrance of the bridge, and heedless of the shaking of the platform caused by so rapid a run, he crosses at full gallop.

In this way he crossed the Beresina, and from his encampment on the right bank, he listened all night to the groans of the poor wretches who lay on its left, crushed by the hoofs of the horses and the wheels of the carts.

But he had escaped, and he returned thanks for Napoleon's genius.

"That passage," he writes some days later, "is a marvel; the result of the Emperor's tactics; the Russians might have done us immense harm."

9

But his troubles were not over.

On the morning of November 28, while Victor fights on the heights above Stoudienka, our Paymaster, still benumbed with cold, makes for Zembin, and the next day, as he goes towards Kamen, he again sees Cossacks circling round the flanks of the column and brandishing their lances.

Through dense forests of birch trees, whose snow-laden branches bend to earth like those of weeping-willows, the army, in mournful silence, steals away from its enemies.

It halts at Iliya, at Molodetchno, at Smorgoni; but the cold is as terrible as ever, and human misery, writes Peyrusse, at its lowest depths. Dead and dying line the roads; some of the soldiers have lost their hearing, some their speech, some their reason; and some with a frenzied laugh approach the bivouac fires and cast themselves into the flames.

Peyrusse is determined not to give way. He hardens himself against the severity of the weather; he swears to keep intact the treasure entrusted to him; for by degrees all the most valuable objects have been locked up in his chest.

He never sleeps now; he urges on his postillions, making up for their apathy and slackness by his own activity and energy; he takes every possible care to get food for his horses; breaks the ice to procure a little water for them to drink, and at night heaps coverings on them to protect them from the cold.

He follows the example of the Emperor, whom he sees daily, and who, he says, in the midst of disaster, shows as the freedom of his mind and the great strength of his character.

"While danger, misfortune, the presence of the enemy, the eternal clamour of the Cossacks press upon us and engross us, Napoleon's energy and elasticity seem only to increase under it all."

10

On the evening of December 5, at Smorgoni, Peyrusse receives a note from Duroc. At eleven o'clock, he is to deliver secretly to the Duc de Frioul a million bills of exchange on the Emperor's account.

At eleven o'clock, he sees the arrival of two carriages, Napoleon with Caulaincourt in one, Duroc with Lobau in the other.

The paymaster hands over the bills of exchange to Duroc, who gives him his instructions. Peyrusse is to hold the same appointment under the King of Naples; the Emperor, who is returning to France, has given over the command to Murat.

"The Emperor," says Peyrusse, "is leaving that he may not witness the death-throes of the army."

And, truly, after Napoleon's departure, the death-agony of the army sets in. For an instant its strength revives, because it counts on finding at Vilna, on December 8, supplies of all sorts, and Peyrusse "crowds on all sail" to get as quickly as possible into the town, which he looks upon as the Promised Land.

But at Vilna, as at Orcha, as at Smolensk, a horrible confusion reigns, and the soldiers seek everywhere for food and shelter in vain.

On December 9 the Cossacks are already at the gates; our troops rush helter-skelter on to the road to Kovno, and Peyrusse, who follows with his fourgon, reaches the foot of the hill of Ponari at ten o'clock.

Ponari is but a wooded slope; but the gradient is steep, the frost makes it impracticable and carts overturned or locked together block the pass.

The whole night long, under twenty-five degrees of cold, Peyrusse tries in vain to climb the hill; neither he nor his horses can keep on their feet. So he resigns himself to camping where he is, though no fires can be lighted lest they should betray the position of the army to the enemy; but he hopes that at last the crowd will pass on, and he relies on being able to get through easily at dawn of day.

Alas! the number of fugitives from Vilna does but increase, and the obstruction grows worse and worse every moment.

How can it be possible in the midst of this throng of men and vehicles—carriages of every kind, guns, wagons, dead horses— to climb the frozen slope of Ponari?

Peyrusse's *fourgon* attempts a step or two, then slips backwards and just escapes falling into a ditch. Far off, from Vilna, echo volleys of firing, and Cossacks make their appearance.

Murat, being consulted, answers that at all costs all the valuables belonging to the Emperor must be saved as far as possible. At once, Peyrusse breaks open his chests and packs gold, *roubles*, jewels and papers into sacks, puts the sacks on horses, giving each horse to one of his servants to lead, sets fire to the fourgon, and sets off on foot.

The confusion of the journey and the darkness of the night disperses the convoy, but next day, at Chichmori, Peyrusse succeeds in getting it together again.[5]

What a rout it was! What a lamentable ending to an expedition! The army now is nothing but a trail of men without arms and wrapped in miserable rags. It evacuates Kovno as it evacuated Vilna, and Peyrusse, on his arrival in the last of the Russian towns, sees, as at Orcha and Smolensk, the shops given over to pillage. In the streets and squares, soldiers, drunk with brandy, and speedily benumbed with cold, pass swiftly from sleep to death.

Peyrusse has put all the contents of his *fourgon* on to a sledge, and when those vile Cossacks, those "devils of madmen," not satisfied with their capture of Ponari, appear, he leaves Kovno; but, instead of attempting the bridge, crowded with fugitives, the sledge where he sits surrounded by his whole "stock" crosses the frozen Niemen.

In this fashion he reached Königsberg; thence, as from headquarters, he made his way to Marienburg, to Marienwerder and to Posen, and it seemed to him that the Prussians were as dangerous as the Cossacks.

His belongings, except a few shirts, and everything he had taken or acquired at Moscow, were lost.

Adieu, pelisses, costly furs, boxes of China tea! *Adieu*, the portrait of the Emperor Alexander, and the hand of the Apostle St. Andrew, that relic Peyrusse had carried off to dazzle his devout female friends with!

---

5. "Your plate and the money in the hands of the paymaster of your household," writes Berthier to Napoleon, "were put into sacks and carried on horses; nothing was lost."

But he himself had escaped; he had not fallen into the hands of the Cossacks. "Could there be a more awful fate than to be a prisoner in twenty-six degrees of cold!" And he had saved his funds.

He had displayed courage, and he was proud of it; a paymaster, a civilian, a *pêkin*, he had not proved "quite a milksop," and he wrote to his brother:

Since the 19th of October, I haven't had a quiet moment; we were disturbed under the gates of Vilna, followed and hunted as far as Bromberg. Nevertheless my health hasn't suffered for an instant; exercise kept away all ailments and, like an oak-tree, water hardened me. You know me to be active and restless, but if you had seen me with a month's beard on me, as dirty as a pig, struggling, running, calling out to the postillions, whipping up the horses, crossing rivers, climbing mountains, forcing my way sword in hand, you would have laughed at the new Don Quixote. I had nothing human left about me but speech; I fed on scraps. I owe keeping my health to this constant moving about, for my hands and feet were never frostbitten but when I had to open my *fourgon* under intense cold, and to empty it, and untie frozen sacks to put my things in; and then to lead my horse and keep his head up lest he should come down.

11

He did not get his reward till fifteen months later, at the conclusion of the French Campaign.

On March 15, 1814, Napoleon made him sub-auditor of the Guard's accounts and Chevalier of the Legion of Honour.

"This accountant," wrote M. de La Bouillerie, paymaster-in-chief to the Crown, to the Emperor, "is upright and intelligent. His conduct on the way back from Russia showed rare zeal and energy; he sacrificed everything he possessed to save your Majesty's papers, accounts, and coffers, of which he has given me an exact account. Many officers of high rank of your Majesty's household deposited their funds with M. Peyrusse and have been repaid in full."

La Bouillerie's testimony was confirmed by that of Daru, the Daru whom Peyrusse called the Grand Patriarch of the Department.

"M. Peyrusse," said Daru, "in the handing in of his accounts, gave proof of a quite scrupulous probity; and, during the Retreat from Moscow, he sacrificed everything that belonged to him to save the treasure, the papers, the jewels of the Emperor, as well as all his accounts."

Peyrusse followed Napoleon to the Island of Elba, and, in 1815, was appointed paymaster-in-chief to the Crown, officer of the Legion of Honour and a baron of the Empire.

After Waterloo, he retired to Carcassonne, his native town.

"What part of the country do you come from?" Murat asked him on December 11, 1812.

"From Carcassonne, Sire."

"Ah!" replied the King of Naples, "that was my first garrison; it is a pretty country."

Peyrusse lived a long time still in that pretty part of the country, for he did not die till 1860, at the age of eighty; and his thoughts often went back to Russia, the Russia into which, as he said, the Grand Army had hurled itself, to be swallowed up.

LEONAUR

ALSO FROM LEONAUR

AVAILABLE IN SOFTCOVER OR HARDCOVER WITH DUST JACKET

WELLINGTON AND THE PYRENEES CAMPAIGN VOLUME I: FROM VITORIA TO THE BIDASSOA *by F. C. Beatson*—The final phase of the campaign in the Iberian Peninsula.

WELLINGTON AND THE INVASION OF FRANCE VOLUME II: THE BIDASSOA TO THE BATTLE OF THE NIVELLE *by F. C. Beatson*—The second of Beatson's series on the fall of Revolutionary France published by Leonaur, the reader is once again taken into the centre of Wellington's strategic and tactical genius.

WELLINGTON AND THE FALL OF FRANCE VOLUME III: THE GAVES AND THE BATTLE OF ORTHEZ *by F. C. Beatson*—This final chapter of F. C. Beatson's brilliant trilogy shows the 'captain of the age' at his most inspired and makes all three books essential additions to any Peninsular War library.

NAVAL BATTLES OF THE NAPOLEONIC WARS *by W. H. Fitchett*—Cape St.Vincent, the Nile, Cadiz, Copenhagen, Trafalgar & Others

SERGEANT GUILLEMARD: THE MAN WHO SHOT NELSON? *by Robert Guillemard*—A Soldier of the Infantry of the French Army of Napoleon on Campaign Throughout Europe

WITH THE GUARDS ACROSS THE PYRENEES by *Robert Batty*—The Experiences of a British Officer of Wellington's Army During the Battles for the Fall of Napoleonic France, 1813.

A STAFF OFFICER IN THE PENINSULA *by E. W. Buckham*—An Officer of the British Staff Corps Cavalry During the Peninsula Campaign of the Napoleonic Wars

THE LEIPZIG CAMPAIGN: 1813—NAPOLEON AND THE "BATTLE OF THE NATIONS" *by F. N. Maude*—Colonel Maude's analysis of Napoleon's campaign of 1813.

BUGEAUD: A PACK WITH A BATON by *Thomas Robert Bugeaud*—The Early Campaigns of a Soldier of Napoleon's Army Who Would Become a Marshal of France.

TWO LEONAUR ORIGINALS

SERGEANT NICOL by *Daniel Nicol*—The Experiences of a Gordon Highlander During the Napoleonic Wars in Egypt, the Peninsula and France.

WATERLOO RECOLLECTIONS by *Frederick Llewellyn*—Rare First Hand Accounts, Letters, Reports and Retellings from the Campaign of 1815.